German Short Stories

Captivating Stories to Learn German & Expand Your Vocabulary the Easy Way

- With the L-R-Method

German - English Parallel Text

by

Edgar Allan Poe

German Translation
Gisela Etzel

Editing and First Chapters © 2018 Beate Ziebell

1

See the end of the book for information on a free audiobook and other bonus material.

Impressum:

Englisches Original: Edgar Allan Poe

Deutsche Übersetzung: Gemeinfrei

Der Originaltext und die Übersetzung ist gemeinfrei. Die Rechte für die zweisprachigen Ausgabe und der einleitenden Kapitel liegen bei:

Beate Ziebell, Schillerstr.94, 15738 Zeuthen

forum-sprachen-lernen.com

info@forum-sprachen-lernen.com

Herstellung und Druck: Siehe Eindruck auf der letzten Seite

ISBN: 9781719803069

Umschlaggestaltung: Beate Ziebell

Introduction

About the creation of these books

A few years ago, I became passionately interested in learning Italian and later French. I was already fluent in English (as a native German speaker), but despite many years of school lessons, I failed in my attempt to learn Russian. Yet even a language as close to German as English, however, I had only really learned after completing school.

With a demanding job and being a single mother, spending hours at school wasn't an option. Moreover, I had also had negative experiences in school in this respect, of course. My son was learning English and French at school. I wanted to convey the experience of speaking a foreign language as being an enrichment. This skill is not only indispensable for careers today, but also opens doors to other cultures!

I was short on time but highly motivated to tackle the problem. There had to be another way of learning languages! One that was easier, faster, more sustainable. How do the best in this field manage to succeed in learning a foreign language, anyway?

These people usually practice quite a "normal" profession and still manage to learn a lot of languages on the side. They don't have much time to learn the foreign language, unlike someone who is dealing with it all day due to their job or even studying the language (such as English). I wanted to learn more about their methods.

One of these methods is the L-R method, which I will describe in greater detail later in the book. I made my first attempts to implement this method when I was looking to support my son learning English. We love the Star Trek series. I turned on the subtitles while watching it and wrote down some lines of dialog. At the same time, I recorded the soundtrack on (back then) a cassette. As a follow-up, we'd always listen to Star Trek at breakfast time. It was great for the learning process – we knew the storyline, my son loved the show and due to the repetitions on the cassette we soon had learned many passages by heart. However, over time, writing down the subtitles proved to be too time-consuming a task in the long run.

I wanted to use the same procedure in French, but in this case, it worked less well. The reason for this was that the French subtitles had very little to do with the spoken French dubbing. You can express the same thing in two very different ways; at least this was the case with the series we tried it with.

And that's how the idea for these books came about. The goal was to identify an exciting text, provide the suitable translation and an audiobook so that the spoken and written word match precisely. What's more, the text and translation should be combined in such a way that the translation can be located particularly quickly. We ultimately ended up listening to "The Red-Headed League", a Sherlock Holmes story. We love Sir Arthur Conan Doyle's language and although it's now several years ago, we still know some passages by heart.

This book is thus the result of our journey in search of good learning material and the right methods for learning languages.

Get ready to be taken into the world of Edgar Allan Poe, learn German at the same time and benefit from the tricks of the best in this field!

Table of Contents

Dear readers!

This book can be used in many ways. On the one hand, you can sit back and relax, read German and, from time to time, let your eyes wander to the translation and brush up your German this way. In this case, you can skip the upcoming chapters about tips for quickly building up your vocabulary, the L-R method and those with many more tips.

Alternately, you can first get an initial overview of the proposed learning methods for effective language learning and the variety of bonus material offered with this book. Try the techniques! You'll be surprised how quickly your reading and listening skills will improve!

What is the quickest way to develop vocabulary?

The L-R Method

As mentioned in the introduction, in order to learn a language, you don't need much more than an interesting text, an easily identifiable suitable translation and an audiobook to learn a language.

Some people who use this method

In her book "How I Learn Languages", Kató Lomp,[1] a Hungarian translator and interpreter who was fluent in 16 languages, described how she quickly expanded her vocabulary by reading foreign-language texts. She didn't even use bilingual editions but translated unfamiliar words using a dictionary.

Phi-Staszek, a Polish multilinguist, improved this method and in the forum "How Do I Learn Any Language" described how you can learn a foreign language within a very short amount of time by only using a bilingual text and an audio recording. He referred to this method as the "L-R method". L-R stands for "Listening-Reading".

---

1   https://de.wikipedia.org/wiki/Kató_Lomb

The American linguist Stephen Krashen[2] describes **extensive reading[3] as the most effective means of language acquisition** and published many articles on the subject. Extensive reading means a lot of reading in a foreign language. With this method, it's not important to understand every word, but to follow the story and find out what happens next. The enjoyment of reading is paramount.

The Oxford University Press ELT also published an article on this topic. It showed that EFL[4] students who **read** a lot do not only learn to read a foreign language **fluently**, but also improve their writing skills in the respective language. According to the study, extensive reading also led to **improved listening skills** and even to a **better active vocabulary**, meaning better speaking skills in the foreign language.

All good reasons for embracing extensive reading and the L-R method!

A practical approach to the L-R method

If an audiobook exists, extensive reading can be more effectively applied to learn a foreign language with the L-R method. Here is the approach for how to learn a great deal within as little time as possible:

1. **First, read the translation** to familiarise yourself with the content of the text. Depending on previous knowledge, this can be one page or maybe even several pages.
2. **Next, listen to the book version and read it in German** at the same time. Try to understand every word and read at the same time. If you can understand everything and read along easily, you can move on to point
3. **Listening without reading**. Maybe even close your eyes. Can you still understand everything? If so, then you can move on to point 4. If not, briefly stop at the places you do not yet understand and look up the unfamiliar word.
4. **Now that you understand the text blindly,** you can **switch to passive listening**. Take the audiobook and listen to it again and again. Set your MP3 player to "repeat indefinitely". It won't hurt to

---

2   https://de.wikipedia.org/wiki/Stephen_Krashen
3   https://oupeltglobalblog.com/2017/01/11/extensive-reading-and-language-learning/
4   EFL= English as a Foreign Language

listen to the whole story over and over again. Then you have already prepared yourself for the next sections and will be faster at points 1 to 3. You will notice that you will soon know many sentences of the text by heart.

Why does the method work?

The amount of text

By reading extensively, you will learn a vast amount of German vocabulary, a plethora of sentence constructions and also, indirectly, about grammar.

Here's an example: Suppose you divide the book "The Red-Headed League" into 30 sections (one section accounts for about 1.5 pages or two minutes of the audiobook). The process of actively going through a part, i.e. the time you actually spend on working out the text with the help of book and audiobook (points 1 to 3 of the L-R method), will not take much longer than 20 minutes (this may take a little longer if there is little or no previous knowledge).

With the commitment of 20 minutes a day, you've worked your way through the entire vocabulary of the Sherlock Holmes story after 30 days, and that's about 1800 different words! Reading can only be learned by reading and this also applies to reading a foreign language. The audiobook contributes to the improvement of listening comprehension and pronunciation.

The layout of the text

By allocating the foreign language to the translation sentence by sentence, the meaning of unknown words can be grasped particularly quickly.

Start the learning with the most common words

Did you know that with the 1000 most-used words[5] of a language you can already understand 76 per cent of a novel's content and about 90 per cent of the spoken language? This was the result of a study by Mark Davies[6]. The percentage varies somewhat from one language to another, but it's an encouraging trend nevertheless. Encouraging because, as shown above, 1000 words can be learned quite fast. This then allows you to move on to content that suits your interests sooner. The meaning of many other words then become apparent from the context without you needing a dictionary.

For this purpose, this book offers a free Anki[7] deck as bonus material for learning the most important German words from various subject areas. Anki is software that is used for the acquisition of vocabulary and other facts. It's free, except for iPhones (it costs about 20 euros to use it on an iPhone). Anki uses its temporal repetition algorithm to ensure that the vocabulary is increasingly anchored in the long-term memory. The "Anki deck" is the name of the different facts to be learned.

Tips for using the Anki deck:

- Learn whole sentences.
- Focus on understanding the word in context (meaning, focus on the extension of the passive vocabulary).
- Take advantage of every opportunity to learn, for example when queuing or commuting to work.

Why learn whole sentences?

A single word can have many meanings. Mark Twain formulated this very aptly in his book "The Awful German Language" with the help of the word "Zug":
Zug: Strictly speaking, "Zug" means: jerk, tug, air flow, procession, march, advance, birds' flight, direction, campaign, railroad, caravan, etc. The real

---

5   http://www.lingref.com/cpp/hls/7/paper1091.pdf
6   http://howlearnspanish.com/2010/08/how-many-words-do-you-need-to-know/
7   https://apps.ankiweb.net/

meaning of "Zug" can thus only be deducted through the context.

For this reason, the deck is not made up of individual terms, but mostly of entire sentences. To read the dialogues, a book in PDF format is available. In the book, there are also gaps to complete as well as their solutions to deepen the knowledge. The Foreign Service Institute created the dialogues. They were drafted for American diplomats who needed to get a handle on the respective country's language as quickly as possible before their stay abroad. If sentences aren't relevant to you, don't hesitate to delete them. Focus on the vocabulary that's important to you. The partially literal translation is particularly positive.

Why should you focus on passive learning?

Again, this is about the amount of vocabulary that you can learn. Adding a word to your passive vocabulary is much faster than adding it to the active vocabulary.

Thus, it's quite possible to increase one's passive vocabulary by a significant amount every day. In contrast, it would only be possible to expand the active vocabulary by a few terms. How much that precisely is, undoubtedly varies from one person to another.

As a general rule, however, the following applies: it is substantially easier to expand the passive vocabulary than it is to develop the active one. The higher the passive vocabulary, the more quickly, and more comprehensively you will be able to read other content. The more time you spend with the foreign language, the greater the extent of your automatic active vocabulary improvement will be. And with this method, you'll do so even faster!

Der Untergang des Hauses Usher - The Fall of the House of Usher

Son coeur est un luth suspendu;
Sitot qu'on le touche il resonne.

DE BERANGER.

During the whole of a dull, dark, and soundless day in the autumn of the year, when the clouds hung oppressively low in the heavens, I had been passing alone, on horseback, through a singularly dreary tract of country;

and at length found myself, as the shades of the evening drew on, within view of the melancholy House of Usher.

I know not how it was--but, with the first glimpse of the building, a sense of insufferable gloom pervaded my spirit.

I say insufferable; for the feeling was unrelieved by any of that half-pleasureable, because poetic, sentiment, with which the mind usually receives even the sternest natural images of the desolate or terrible.

I looked upon the scene before me--upon the mere house, and the simple landscape features of the domain--upon the bleak walls--upon the vacant eye-like windows--upon a few rank sedges--and upon a few white trunks of decayed trees--

with an utter depression of soul which I can compare to no earthly sensation more properly than to the after-dream of the reveller upon opium--the bitter lapse into everyday life--the hideous dropping off of the veil.

There was an iciness, a sinking, a

Son coeur est un luth suspendu;
Sitôt qu'on le touche il résonne.

De Beranger

Ich war den ganzen Tag lang geritten, einen grauen und lautlosen melancholischen Herbsttag lang – durch eine eigentümlich öde und traurige Gegend, auf die erdrückend schwer die Wolken herabhingen.

Da endlich, als die Schatten des Abends herniedersanken, sah ich das Stammschloss der Usher vor mir.

Ich weiß nicht, wie es kam – aber ich wurde gleich beim ersten Anblick dieser Mauern von einem unerträglich trüben Gefühl befallen.

Ich sage unerträglich, denn dies Gefühl wurde durch keine der poetischen und darum erleichternden Empfindungen gelindert, mit denen die Seele gewöhnlich selbst die finstersten Bilder des Trostlosen oder Schaurigen aufnimmt.

Ich betrachtete das Bild vor mir – das einsame Gebäude in seiner einförmigen Umgebung, die kahlen Mauern, die toten, wie leere Augenhöhlen starrenden Fenster, die paar Büschel dürrer Binsen, die weißschimmernden Stümpfe abgestorbener Bäume –

mit einer Niedergeschlagenheit, die ich mit keinem anderen Gefühl besser vergleichen kann als mit dem trostlosen Erwachen eines Opiumessers aus seinem Rausche, dem bitteren Zurücksinnen in graue Alltagswirklichkeit, wenn der verklärende Schleier unerbittlich zerreißt.

Es war ein frostiges Erstarren, ein

sickening of the heart--an unredeemed dreariness of thought which no goading of the imagination could torture into aught of the sublime.

What was it--I paused to think--what was it that so unnerved me in the contemplation of the House of Usher?

It was a mystery all insoluble; nor could I grapple with the shadowy fancies that crowded upon me as I pondered.

I was forced to fall back upon the unsatisfactory conclusion, that while, beyond doubt, there are combinations of very simple natural objects which have the power of thus affecting us, still the analysis of this power lies among considerations beyond our depth.

It was possible, I reflected, that a mere different arrangement of the particulars of the scene, of the details of the picture, would be sufficient to modify, or perhaps to annihilate its capacity for sorrowful impression; and,

acting upon this idea, I reined my horse to the precipitous brink of a black and lurid tarn that lay in unruffled lustre by the dwelling, and gazed down--

but with a shudder even more thrilling than before--upon the remodelled and inverted images of the grey sedge, and the ghastly tree-stems, and the vacant and eye-like windows.

Nevertheless, in this mansion of gloom I now proposed to myself a sojourn of some weeks.

Its proprietor, Roderick Usher, had been one of my boon companions in boyhood;

Erliegen aller Lebenskraft – kurz, eine hilflose Traurigkeit der Gedanken, die kein noch so gewaltsames Anstacheln der Einbildungskraft aufreizen konnte zu Erhabenheit, zu Größe.

Was mochte es sein – dachte ich, langsamer reitend –, ja, was mochte es sein, dass der Anblick des Hauses Usher mich so erschreckend überwältigte?

Es war mir ein Rätsel; aber ich konnte mich der grauen Wahngespenster nicht erwehren;

ich musste mich mit der wenig befriedigenden Erklärung begnügen, dass es tatsächlich in der Natur ganz einfache Dinge gibt, die durch die Umstände, in denen sie uns erscheinen, geradezu niederdrückend auf uns wirken können, dass es aber nicht in unsere Macht gegeben ist, eine Definition dieser Gewalt zu finden.

Es wäre möglich, überlegte ich, dass eine etwas andere Anordnung der einzelnen Bestandteile dieses Landschaftsbildes genügen würde, um die düstere Stimmung des Ganzen abzuschwächen, ja vielleicht sogar vollständig aufzuheben.

Von diesem Gedanken getrieben, lenkte ich mein Pferd an den steilen Abhang eines schwarzen sumpfigen Teiches, der von keinem Hauch bewegt neben dem Schlosse lag, und spähte ins Wasser –

doch ein Schauder, stärker als zuvor, schüttelte mich beim Anblick der auf den Kopf gestellten und verzerrten Bilder der grauen Binsen, der gespenstischen Baumstümpfe und der toten, wie leere Augenhöhlen starrenden Fenster.

Nichtsdestoweniger beschloss ich, in diesem schwermutvollen Hause einen Aufenthalt von mehreren Wochen zu nehmen.

Sein Eigentümer, Roderick Usher, war einer meiner liebsten Jugendfreunde

but many years had elapsed since our last meeting.

A letter, however, had lately reached me in a distant part of the country--a letter from him--which, in its wildly importunate nature, had admitted of no other than a personal reply.

The MS gave evidence of nervous agitation.

The writer spoke of acute bodily illness--of a mental disorder which oppressed him--and of an earnest desire to see me, as his best, and indeed his only personal friend, with a view of attempting, by the cheerfulness of my society, some alleviation of his malady.

It was the manner in which all this, and much more, was said--it was the apparent heart that went with his request--which allowed me no room for hesitation; and I accordingly obeyed forthwith what I still considered a very singular summons.

Although, as boys, we had been even intimate associates, yet I really knew little of my friend.

His reserve had been always excessive and habitual.

I was aware, however, that his very ancient family had been noted, time out of mind, for a peculiar sensibility of temperament, displaying itself, through long ages, in many works of exalted art,

and manifested, of late, in repeated deeds of munificent yet unobtrusive charity, as

gewesen, doch seit unserer letzten Begegnung waren viele Jahre dahingegangen.

Da hatte mich jüngst bei meinem Aufenthalt in einem entlegenen Teil des Landes ein Brief erreicht – ein Brief von ihm –, dessen seltsam ungestümer Charakter keine andere als eine persönliche und mündliche Beantwortung zuließ.

Das Schreiben zeugte entschieden von nervöser Aufregung.

Der Verfasser sprach von einer heftigen körperlichen Erkrankung – von niederdrückender geistiger Zerrüttung – und von dem innigen Wunsch, mich, der ich sein bester und tatsächlich sein einziger persönlicher Freund sei, wiederzusehen; er hoffe, meine erheiternde Gesellschaft werde seinem Zustande etwas Erleichterung bringen.

Die Art und Weise, in der dies und vieles andere gesagt war – die Herzensbedrängnis, die aus seinem Verlangen sprach –, das war es, das mir kein Zögern erlaubte, und ich gehorchte daher dieser höchst seltsamen Aufforderung unverzüglich.

Obgleich wir als Knaben geradezu vertraute Kameraden gewesen waren, wusste ich dennoch recht wenig über meinen Freund.

Seine Zurückhaltung war immer außerordentlich gewesen; sie war ihm ganz selbstverständlich erschienen.

Immerhin war mir bekannt, dass seine sehr alte Familie seit undenklichen Zeiten wegen einer eigentümlichen Reizbarkeit des Temperaments bekannt gewesen war, einer Reizbarkeit, die lange Jahre hindurch in vielen erhaben eigenartigen Kunstwerken sich aussprach;

später betätigte sich dies feinfühlige Empfinden in mancher Handlung

well as in a passionate devotion to the intricacies, perhaps even more than to the orthodox and easily recognisable beauties of musical science.

I had learned, too, the very remarkable fact, that the stem of the Usher race, all time-honoured as it was, had put forth, at no period, any enduring branch; in other words, that the entire family lay in the direct line of descent, and had always, with very trifling and very temporary variation, so lain.

It was this deficiency, I considered, while running over in thought the perfect keeping of the character of the premises with the accredited character of the people, and while speculating upon the possible influence which the one, in the long lapse of centuries, might have exercised upon the other--it was this deficiency,

perhaps, of collateral issue, and the consequent undeviating transmission, from sire to son, of the patrimony with the name, which had, at length, so identified the two as to merge the original title of the estate in the quaint and equivocal appellation of the "House of Usher"--

an appellation which seemed to include, in the minds of the peasantry who used it, both the family and the family mansion.

I have said that the sole effect of my somewhat childish experiment--that of looking down within the tarn--had been to deepen the first singular impression.

großmütiger, doch unauffälliger Mildtätigkeit und in der leidenschaftlichen Hingabe an das Studium der Musik – weniger also an ihre altbekannten leichtfasslichen Schönheitsformen, als an die tiefverborgenen Probleme dieser Kunst.

Ich hatte auch die sehr bemerkenswerte Tatsache erfahren, dass der Stammbaum der Familie Usher, die jederzeit hochangesehen gewesen, zu keiner Zeit einen ausdauernden Nebenzweig hervorgebracht hatte, mit anderen Worten, dass die Abstammung der ganzen Familie in direkter Linie herzustellen war.

Und ich vergegenwärtigte mir, dass in dieser Familie neben dem ungeteilten Besitztum auch die besonderen Charaktereigentümlichkeiten sich ungeteilt von Glied zu Glied vererbten, und sann darüber nach, inwieweit im Laufe der Jahrhunderte die eine dieser Tatsachen die andere beeinflusst haben könne.

Wahrscheinlich, so sagte ich mir, ist es eben dieser Mangel einer Seitenlinie, ist es dies von Vater zu Sohn immer sich gleichbleibende Erbe von Besitztum und Familienname, das schließlich beide so miteinander identifiziert hatte, dass der ursprüngliche Name des Besitztums in die wunderliche und doppeldeutige Bezeichnung ›das Haus Usher‹ übergegangen war –

eine Benennung, die bei den Bauern, die sie anwendeten, beides, sowohl die Familie wie das Familienhaus, zu bezeichnen schien.

Ich sagte vorhin, dass der einzige Erfolg meines etwas kindischen Beginnens – meines Hinabblickens in den dunklen Teich – der gewesen war, den ersten sonderbaren Eindruck, den das Landschaftsbild auf mich gemacht hatte,

noch zu vertiefen.

There can be no doubt that the consciousness of the rapid increase of my superstition--for why should I not so term it?--served mainly to accelerate the increase itself.

Es ist zweifellos: das Bewusstsein, mit dem ich das Anwachsen meiner abergläubischen Furcht – denn dies ist der rechte Name für die Sache – verfolgte, diente nur dazu, diese Furcht selbst zu steigern.

Such, I have long known, is the paradoxical law of all sentiments having terror as a basis.

Denn ich kannte schon lange das paradoxe Gesetz aller Empfindungen, deren Ursprung das Entsetzen, das Grauen ist.

And it might have been for this reason only, that, when I again uplifted my eyes to the house itself, from its image in the pool, there grew in my mind a strange fancy--

Und einzig dies mag die Ursache gewesen sein einer seltsamen Vorstellung, die in meiner Seele entstand, als ich meine Augen von dem Spiegelbild im Pfuhl wieder hinaufrichtete auf das Wohnhaus selbst;

a fancy so ridiculous, indeed, that I but mention it to show the vivid force of the sensations which oppressed me.

es war eine Einbildung, so lächerlich in der Tat, dass ich sie nur erwähne, um zu zeigen, wie lebendig, wie stark die Eindrücke waren, die auf mir lasteten.

I had so worked upon my imagination as really to believe that about the whole mansion and domain there hung an atmosphere peculiar to themselves and their immediate vicinity--

Ich hatte so auf meine Einbildungskraft eingearbeitet, dass ich wirklich glaubte, das Haus und seine ganze Umgebung sei von einer nur ihm eigentümlichen Atmosphäre umflutet –

an atmosphere which had no affinity with the air of heaven, but which had reeked up from the decayed trees, and the grey wall, and the silent tarn--a pestilent and mystic vapour, dull, sluggish, faintly discernible, and leaden-hued.

einer Atmosphäre, die zu der Himmelsluft keinerlei Zugehörigkeit hatte, sondern die emporgedunstet war aus den vermorschten Bäumen, den grauen Mauern und dem stummen Pfuhl – ein giftiger, geheimnisvoller, trüber, träger, kaum wahrnehmbarer bleifarbener Dunst.

Shaking off from my spirit what must have been a dream, I scanned more narrowly the real aspect of the building.

Von meinem Geist abschüttelnd, was Traum gewesen sein musste, prüfte ich eingehender das wirkliche Aussehen des Gebäudes.

Its principal feature seemed to be that of an excessive antiquity.

Das auffallendste an ihm schien mir sein beträchtliches Alter zu sein.

The discoloration of ages had been great.

Die Zeit hatten ihm seine ursprüngliche Farbe genommen.

Minute fungi overspread the whole exterior, hanging in a fine tangled web-

Ein winzig kleiner Pilz hatte alle Mauern wie mit einem Netzwerk überzogen,

work from the eaves.

Yet all this was apart from any extraordinary dilapidation.

No portion of the masonry had fallen; and there appeared to be a wild inconsistency between its still perfect adaptation of parts, and the crumbling condition of the individual stones.

In this there was much that reminded me of the specious totality of old wood-work which has rotted for long years in some neglected vault, with no disturbance from the breath of the external air.

Beyond this indication of extensive decay, however, the fabric gave little token of instability.

Perhaps the eye of a scrutinizing observer might have discovered a barely perceptible fissure, which, extending from the roof of the building in front, made its way down the wall in a zigzag direction, until it became lost in the sullen waters of the tarn.

Noticing these things, I rode over a short causeway to the house.

A servant in waiting took my horse, and I entered the Gothic archway of the hall.

A valet, of stealthy step, thence conducted me, in silence, through many dark and intricate passages in my progress to the studio of his master.

Much that I encountered on the way contributed, I know not how, to heighten the vague sentiments of which I have already spoken.

While the objects around me--while the carvings of the ceilings, the sombre tapestries of the walls, the ebon

dessen feinmaschiges Geflecht von den Dachtraufen herabhing.

Doch von irgendwelchem außergewöhnlichen Verfall war das Gebäude noch weit entfernt.

Kein Teil des Mauerwerks war eingesunken, und die noch vollkommen erhaltene Gesamtheit stand in seltsamem Widerspruch zu der bröckelnden Schadhaftigkeit der einzelnen Steine.

Dies Haus stand gleichsam da wie altes Holzgetäfel, das in irgendeinem unbetretenen Gewölbe viele Jahre lang vermoderte, ohne dass je ein Lufthauch von draußen es berührte, und das darum in all seinem inneren Verfall stattlich und lückenlos dasteht.

Außer diesen Zeichen eines allgemeinen Verfalls bot das Haus jedoch nur wenige Merkmale von Baufälligkeit.

Vielleicht hätte allerdings ein scharfprüfender Blick einen kaum wahrnehmbaren Riss entdecken können, der an der Frontseite des Hauses vom Dach im Zickzack die Mauer hinunterlief, bis er sich in den trüben Wassern des Teiches verlor.

Diese Dinge bemerkte ich, während ich über einen kurzen Dammweg zum Hause hinauffritt.

Ein wartender Diener nahm mein Pferd, und ich trat unter den gotisch gewölbten Torbogen der Halle.

Ein Kammerdiener mit leichtem, leisem Schritt führte mich schweigend durch dunkle und gewundene Gänge bis in das Arbeitszimmer seines Herrn.

Vieles, was ich unterwegs erblickte, trug irgendwie dazu bei, das unbestimmte niederdrückende Gefühl, von dem ich schon gesprochen habe, zu verstärken.

Diese Dinge um mich her – das Schnitzwerk der Deckentäfelung, der ebenholzglänzende Flur, die düsteren

blackness of the floors, and the phantasmagoric armorial trophies which rattled as I strode,

were but matters to which, or to such as which, I had been accustomed from my infancy--while I hesitated not to acknowledge how familiar was all this--I still wondered to find how unfamiliar were the fancies which ordinary images were stirring up.

On one of the staircases, I met the physician of the family.

His countenance, I thought, wore a mingled expression of low cunning and perplexity.

He accosted me with trepidation and passed on.

The valet now threw open a door and ushered me into the presence of his master.

The room in which I found myself was very large and lofty.

The windows were long, narrow, and pointed, and at so vast a distance from the black oaken floor as to be altogether inaccessible from within.

Feeble gleams of encrimsoned light made their way through the trellised panes, and served to render sufficiently distinct the more prominent objects around; the eye, however, struggled in vain to reach the remoter angles of the chamber, or the recesses of the vaulted and fretted ceiling.

Dark draperies hung upon the walls.

The general furniture was profuse, comfortless, antique, and tattered.

Many books and musical instruments lay scattered about, but failed to give any vitality to the scene.

Wandteppiche mit ihrem phantastischen Waffenschmuck, der bei meinen Tritten rasselte –,

das alles waren Dinge, die schon meiner Kindheit vertraut gewesen waren, wie ich mir unumwunden eingestehen musste –, dennoch wunderte ich mich, was für unheimliche Vorstellungen so gewöhnliche Dinge erwecken konnten.

Auf einer der Treppen begegnete ich dem Hausarzt.

Sein Gesichtsausdruck erschien mir gemein und durchtrieben, obgleich mein Anblick ihn verblüffte.

Er begrüßte mich verwirrt und ging weiter.

Jetzt riss der Kammerdiener eine Türe auf und führte mich hinein zu seinem Herrn.

Das Zimmer, in dem ich mich nun befand, war sehr groß und hoch.

Die Fenster waren lang und schmal und hatten gotische Spitzbogenform; sie befanden sich so hoch über dem schwarzen eichenen Fußboden, dass man nicht an sie heranreichen konnte.

Ein schwacher Schimmer rötlichen Lichtes drang durch die vergitterten Scheiben herein und reichte gerade hin, die hervortretenden Gegenstände des Gemachs erkennbar zu machen; doch mühte sich das Auge vergebens, bis in die entfernten Winkel des Zimmers oder in die Tiefen der schmuckreichen Deckenwölbung vorzudringen.

Dunkle Teppiche hingen an den Wänden.

Die Einrichtung war im allgemeinen überladen prunkvoll, unbehaglich, altmodisch und schadhaft.

Eine Menge Bücher und Musikinstrumente lagen umher, doch auch das vermochte nicht, die tote Starrheit des öden Raumes zu beleben.

I felt that I breathed an atmosphere of sorrow.

An air of stern, deep, and irredeemable gloom hung over and pervaded all.

Upon my entrance, Usher rose from a sofa on which he had been lying at full length, and greeted me with a vivacious warmth which had much in it, I at first thought, of an overdone cordiality--of the constrained effort of the ennuye man of the world.

A glance, however, at his countenance, convinced me of his perfect sincerity.

We sat down; and for some moments, while he spoke not, I gazed upon him with a feeling half of pity, half of awe.

Surely, man had never before so terribly altered, in so brief a period, as had Roderick Usher!

It was with difficulty that I could bring myself to admit the identity of the wan being before me with the companion of my early boyhood.

Yet the character of his face had been at all times remarkable.

A cadaverousness of complexion; an eye large, liquid, and luminous beyond comparison; lips somewhat thin and very pallid, but of a surpassingly beautiful curve; a nose of a delicate Hebrew model, but with a breadth of nostril unusual in similar formations;

a finely-moulded chin, speaking, in its want of prominence, of a want of moral energy; hair of a more than web-like softness and tenuity;

these features, with an inordinate expansion above the regions of the temple, made up altogether a countenance not easily to be forgotten.

And now in the mere exaggeration of the prevailing character of these features,

Ich fühlte, dass ich eine Luft einatmete, die schwer von Gram und Sorge war.

Wie ernste, tiefe, unheilbare Schwermut lastete es hier auf allem.

Bei meinem Eintritt erhob sich Usher von einem Sofa, auf dem er lang ausgestreckt gelegen hatte, und begrüßte mich mit warmer Lebhaftigkeit, die mir zuerst übertrieben schien – etwa als gezwungene Liebenswürdigkeit des blasierten Weltmannes.

Ein Blick jedoch auf sein Gesicht überzeugte mich von seiner völligen Aufrichtigkeit.

Wir setzten uns, und da er nicht gleich sprach, betrachtete ich ihn minutenlang – und wurde von Mitleid und Grauen ergriffen.

Sicherlich, kein Mensch hatte sich je in so kurzer Zeit so schrecklich verändert wie Roderick Usher!

Nur mit Mühe gelang es mir, die Identität dieser gespenstischen Gestalt da vor mir mit dem Gefährten meiner Kindheit festzustellen.

Doch seine Gesichtsbildung war immer merkwürdig und auffallend gewesen:

eine leichenhafte Blässe; große klare und unvergleichlich leuchtende Augen; Lippen, die etwas schmal und sehr bleich waren – aber von ungemein schönem Schwunge; eine Nase von edelzartem jüdischen Schnitt, doch mit ungewöhnlich breiten Nüstern;

ein schöngebildetes Kinn, dessen wenig kräftige Form einen Mangel an sittlicher Energie verriet; Haare, die feiner und zarter waren als Spinnenfäden.

Diese einzelnen Züge, verbunden mit einer massigen Kraft und Breite der Stirn über den Schläfen, bildeten ein Antlitz, das man nicht leicht vergessen konnte.

Und nun hatte die übertriebene Entwicklung dieser charakteristischen

and of the expression they were wont to convey, lay so much of change that I doubted to whom I spoke.

The now ghastly pallor of the skin, and the now miraculous lustre of the eye, above all things startled and even awed me.

The silken hair, too, had been suffered to grow all unheeded, and as, in its wild gossamer texture, it floated rather than fell about the face, I could not, even with effort, connect its Arabesque expression with any idea of simple humanity.

In the manner of my friend I was at once struck with an incoherence--an inconsistency; and I soon found this to arise from a series of feeble and futile struggles to overcome an habitual trepidancy--an excessive nervous agitation.

For something of this nature I had indeed been prepared, no less by his letter, than by reminiscences of certain boyish traits, and by conclusions deduced from his peculiar physical conformation and temperament.

His action was alternately vivacious and sullen.

His voice varied rapidly from a tremulous indecision (when the animal spirits seemed utterly in abeyance) to that species of energetic concision--that abrupt, weighty, unhurried, and hollow-sounding enunciation--

that leaden, self-balanced and perfectly modulated guttural utterance, which may be observed in the lost drunkard, or the

Einzelheiten genügt, den Ausdruck seiner Züge derart zu verändern, dass ich nicht einmal wusste, ob er es wirklich war.

Vor allem war ich bestürzt, ja entsetzt von der jetzt gespenstischen Blässe der Haut und dem jetzt übernatürlichen Strahlen des Auges.

Das seidige Haar hatte ein ungewöhnliches Wachstum entfaltet, und wie es da so seltsam wie hauchzarter Altweibersommer sein Gesicht umflutete, konnte ich beim besten Willen nicht dies arabeskenhaft verschlungene Gewebe mit dem einfachen Begriff Menschenhaar in Beziehung bringen.

Im Benehmen meines Freundes überraschte mich sofort eine gewisse Verwirrtheit – seiner Rede fehlte der Zusammenhang; und ich erkannte dies als eine Folge seiner wiederholten kraftlosen Versuche, ein ihm innewohnendes Angstgefühl, das ihn wie Zittern überkam, zu unterdrücken – einer heftigen nervösen Aufregung Herr zu werden.

Ich war allerdings auf etwas Derartiges gefasst gewesen; sowohl sein Brief als auch meine Erinnerung an bestimmte Wesenseigenheiten des Knaben hatten mich darauf vorbereitet, und auch sein Äußeres wie sein Temperament ließen dergleichen ahnen.

Sein Wesen war abwechselnd lebhaft und mürrisch.

Seine Stimme, die eben noch zitternd und unsicher war (wenn die Lebensgeister in tödlicher Erschlaffung ruhten), flammte plötzlich auf zu heftiger Entschiedenheit – wurde schroff und nachdrücklich – dann schwerfällig und dumpf, bleiern einfältig –

wurde zu den sonderbar modulierten Kehllauten der ungeheuren Aufregung des sinnlos Betrunkenen oder des

irreclaimable eater of opium, during the periods of his most intense excitement.

It was thus that he spoke of the object of my visit, of his earnest desire to see me, and of the solace he expected me to afford him.

He entered, at some length, into what he conceived to be the nature of his malady.

It was, he said, a constitutional and a family evil, and one for which he despaired to find a remedy--a mere nervous affection, he immediately added, which would undoubtedly soon pass off.

It displayed itself in a host of unnatural sensations.

Some of these, as he detailed them, interested and bewildered me; although, perhaps, the terms, and the general manner of the narration had their weight.

He suffered much from a morbid acuteness of the senses; the most insipid food was alone endurable; he could wear only garments of certain texture;

the odours of all flowers were oppressive; his eyes were tortured by even a faint light; and there were but peculiar sounds, and these from stringed instruments, which did not inspire him with horror.

To an anomalous species of terror I found him a bounden slave.

"I shall perish," said he, "I must perish in this deplorable folly.

Thus, thus, and not otherwise, shall I be lost.

I dread the events of the future, not in themselves, but in their results.

I shudder at the thought of any, even the most trivial, incident, which may operate

unverbesserlichen Opiumessers.

So sprach er also von dem Zweck meines Besuches, von seinem dringenden Verlangen, mich zu sehen, und von dem trostreichen Einfluss, den er von mir erhoffe.

Nach einer Weile kam er auf die Natur seiner Krankheit zu sprechen.

Es war, sagte er, ein ererbtes Familienübel, ein Übel, für das ein Heilmittel zu finden er verzweifle – nichts weiter als nervöse Angegriffenheit, fügte er sofort hinzu, die zweifellos bald vorübergehen werde.

Sie äußere sich in einer Menge unnatürlicher Erregungszustände.

Einige derselben, die er mir nun beschrieb, verblüfften und erschreckten mich, doch mochte an dieser Wirkung seine Ausdrucksweise, die Form seines Berichtes, schuld sein.

Er litt viel unter einer krankhaften Verschärfung der Sinne; nur die fadeste Nahrung war ihm erträglich; als Kleidung konnte er nur ganz bestimmte Stoffe tragen;

jeglicher Blumenduft war ihm zuwider; selbst das schwächste Licht quälte seine Augen, und es gab nur einige besondere Tonklänge – und diese nur von Saiteninstrumenten –, die ihn nicht mit Entsetzen erfüllten.

Ich sah, dass er der Furcht, dem Schreck, dem Grauen sklavisch unterworfen war.

"Ich werde zugrunde gehen", sagte er, "ich muss zugrunde gehen an dieser beklagenswerten Narrheit.

So, so und nicht anders wird mich der Untergang ereilen!

Ich fürchte die Ereignisse der Zukunft – nicht sie selbst, aber ihre Wirkungen.

Ich schaudere bei dem Gedanken, irgendein ganz geringfügiger Vorfall

upon this intolerable agitation of soul.

I have, indeed, no abhorrence of danger, except in its absolute effect--in terror.

In this unnerved--in this pitiable condition--I feel that the period will sooner or later arrive when I must abandon life and reason together, in some struggle with the grim phantasm, FEAR."

I learned, moreover, at intervals, and through broken and equivocal hints, another singular feature of his mental condition.

He was enchained by certain superstitious impressions in regard to the dwelling which he tenanted,

and whence, for many years, he had never ventured forth--in regard to an influence whose supposititious force was conveyed in terms too shadowy here to be re-stated--

an influence which some peculiarities in the mere form and substance of his family mansion, had, by dint of long sufferance, he said, obtained over his spirit--an effect which the physique of the grey walls and turrets, and of the dim tarn into which they all looked down, had, at length, brought about upon the morale of his existence.

He admitted, however, although with hesitation, that much of the peculiar gloom which thus afflicted him could be traced to a more natural and far more palpable origin--to the severe and long-continued illness--indeed to the evidently approaching dissolution--of a tenderly beloved sister--his sole companion for long years--his last and only relative on earth.

könne die unerträgliche Seelenerregung verschlimmern.

Ich habe wirklich kein Entsetzen vor der Gefahr, nur vor ihrer unvermeidlichen Wirkung – vor dem Schrecken.

In diesem entnervten, in diesem bedauernswerten Zustand fühle ich, dass früher oder später die Zeit kommen wird, da ich beides, Vernunft und Leben, hingeben muss – verlieren im Kampf mit dem grässlichen Phantom: Furcht.

"Noch einen andern sonderbaren Zug seiner geistigen Verfassung erfuhr ich nach und nach aus abgerissenen, unbestimmten Andeutungen.

Er war hinsichtlich des Hauses, das er bewohnte, in gewissen abergläubischen Vorstellungen befangen.

Schon seit Jahren hatte er sich nicht mehr aus dem Hause herausgewagt – infolge eines Einflusses, dessen eingebildete Wirkung er mir in so unbestimmten, schattendunkeln Worten mitteilte, dass ich sie hier nicht wiedergeben kann.

Wie er sagte, hatten einige Besonderheiten in der Bauart und dem Baumaterial seines Stammschlosses in dieser langen Leidenszeit auf seinen Geist Einfluss erlangt – einen Einfluss also, den das Physische der grauen Mauern und Türme und des trüben Pfuhls, in den sie alle hinabstarrten, auf seine Psyche ausübte.

Jedoch gab er zögernd zu, dass die seltsame Schwermut, unter der er leide, einer natürlicheren, gewissermaßen handgreiflicheren Ursache zugeschrieben werden könne – nämlich der schweren und langwierigen Krankheit – ja der offenbar nahen Auflösung – einer zärtlich geliebten Schwester – der einzigen Gefährtin langer Jahre – der letzten und einzigen Verwandten auf Erden.

"Her decease," he said, with a bitterness which I can never forget, "would leave him (him the hopeless and the frail) the last of the ancient race of the Ushers."

While he spoke, the lady Madeline (for so was she called) passed slowly through a remote portion of the apartment, and, without having noticed my presence, disappeared.

I regarded her with an utter astonishment not unmingled with dread--and yet I found it impossible to account for such feelings.

A sensation of stupor oppressed me, as my eyes followed her retreating steps.

When a door, at length, closed upon her, my glance sought instinctively and eagerly the countenance of the brother-- but he had buried his face in his hands, and I could only perceive that a far more than ordinary wanness had overspread the emaciated fingers through which trickled many passionate tears.

The disease of the lady Madeline had long baffled the skill of her physicians.

A settled apathy, a gradual wasting away of the person, and frequent although transient affections of a partially cataleptical character, were the unusual diagnosis.

Hitherto she had steadily borne up against the pressure of her malady, and had not betaken herself finally to bed; but, on the closing in of the evening of my arrival at the house, she succumbed (as her brother told me at night with inexpressible agitation) to the prostrating power of the destroyer; and I learned that the glimpse I had obtained of her person

Ihr Hinscheiden, sagte er mit einer Bitterkeit, die ich nie vergessen kann, würde ihn (ihn, den Hoffnungslosen, Gebrechlichen) als den Letzten des alten Geschlechtes der Usher zurücklassen.

Während er sprach, durchschritt Lady Magdalen – so hieß seine Schwester – langsam den entfernten Teil des Gemachs und verschwand, ohne meine Anwesenheit beachtet zu haben.

Ich betrachtete sie mit maßlosem Erstaunen, das nicht frei war von Entsetzen – und dennoch konnte ich mir keine Rechenschaft geben über das, was ich fühlte.

Wie Erstarrung kam es über mich, als meine Augen ihren entschwebenden Schritten folgten.

Als sich die Tür hinter ihr geschlossen hatte, suchte mein Blick unwillkürlich und begierig das Antlitz des Bruders – aber er hatte das Gesicht in den Händen vergraben, und ich konnte nur bemerken, dass seine mageren Finger, zwischen denen viele leidenschaftliche Tränen hindurchsickerten, von noch gespenstischerer Blässe waren als gewöhnlich.

Schon lange hatte die Krankheit der Lady Magdalen der Geschicklichkeit der Ärzte gespottet.

Eine beständige Apathie, ein langsames Hinwelken und häufige, wenn auch vorübergehende Anfälle, vermutlich kataleptischer Natur, das war die ungewöhnliche Diagnose.

Bislang hatte sie standhaft der Gewalt der Krankheit getrotzt und war noch nicht bettlägerig geworden.

Am Tage meiner Ankunft aber unterlag sie gegen Abend der vernichtenden Macht des Zerstörers – so berichtete ihr Bruder mir des Nachts in unaussprechlicher Aufregung, und ich erfuhr, dass der flüchtige Anblick, den

would thus probably be the last I should obtain--that the lady, at least while living, would be seen by me no more.

For several days ensuing, her name was unmentioned by either Usher or myself: and during this period I was busied in earnest endeavours to alleviate the melancholy of my friend.

We painted and read together; or I listened, as if in a dream, to the wild improvisations of his speaking guitar.

And thus, as a closer and still closer intimacy admitted me more unreservedly into the recesses of his spirit, the more bitterly did I perceive the futility of all attempt at cheering a mind from which darkness, as if an inherent positive quality, poured forth upon all objects of the moral and physical universe, in one unceasing radiation of gloom.

I shall ever bear about me a memory of the many solemn hours I thus spent alone with the master of the House of Usher.

Yet I should fail in any attempt to convey an idea of the exact character of the studies, or of the occupations, in which he involved me, or led me the way.

An excited and highly distempered ideality threw a sulphureous lustre over all. His long improvised dirges will ring for ever in my ears.

Among other things, I hold painfully in mind a certain singular perversion and amplification of the wild air of the last waltz of Von Weber.

ich von ihr gehabt, wohl auch der letzte gewesen sein werde – dass Lady Magdalen wenigstens lebend nicht mehr von mir erblickt würde.

In den nächsten Tagen wurde ihr Name weder von Usher noch von mir erwähnt; und während dieser Zeit war ich ernstlich und angestrengt bemüht, meinen Freund seinem Trübsinn zu entreißen.

Wir malten und lasen zusammen, oder ich lauschte wie im Traum seinen seltsamen Improvisationen auf der Gitarre.

Und wie nun eine innige und immer innigere Vertrautheit mich immer rückhaltloser eindringen ließ in die Tiefen seiner Seele, kam ich immer mehr zu der bitteren Erkenntnis, dass alle Versuche vergeblich sein mussten, ein Gemüt zu erheitern, dessen Schwermut wie eine ewig unwandelbare positive Eigenschaft sich ergoss und alle Dinge der Welt stetig und ausnahmslos mit düsteren Strahlen beflutete.

Ich werde stets ein Andenken bewahren an die vielen feierlich ernsten Stunden, die ich so allein mit dem Haupt des Hauses Usher zubrachte;

dennoch ist es mir nicht möglich, einen Begriff zu geben von dem Charakter der Studien oder Beschäftigungen, in die er mich einspann oder zu denen er mich hinwies.

Sein übertriebener, ruheloser, geradezu krankhafter Idealismus warf auf all unser Tun einen schwefelig feurigen Glanz.

Seine langen improvisierten Klagegesänge werden mir ewig in den Ohren klingen; unter anderem habe ich in schmerzlichster, quälendster Erinnerung eine seltsame Variation – eine Paraphrase über ›Carl Maria von Webers letzte Gedanken‹.

From the paintings over which his elaborate fancy brooded, and which grew, touch by touch, into vagueness at which I shuddered the more thrillingly, because I shuddered knowing not why;-- from these paintings (vivid as their images now are before me)

I would in vain endeavour to educe more than a small portion which should lie within the compass of merely written words.

By the utter simplicity, by the nakedness of his designs, he arrested and overawed attention.

If ever mortal painted an idea, that mortal was Roderick Usher.

For me at least--in the circumstances then surrounding me--there arose out of the pure abstractions which the hypochondriac contrived to throw upon his canvas, an intensity of intolerable awe, no shadow of which felt I ever yet in the contemplation of the certainly glowing yet too concrete reveries of Fuseli.

One of the phantasmagoric conceptions of my friend, partaking not so rigidly of the spirit of abstraction, may be shadowed forth, although feebly, in words.

A small picture presented the interior of an immensely long and rectangular vault or tunnel, with low walls, smooth, white, and without interruption or device.

Certain accessory points of the design served well to convey the idea that this excavation lay at an exceeding depth below the surface of the earth.

Die Bildwerke, die seine rastlose Phantasie erstehen ließ und die seine Hand in wunderbar verschwommenen Strichen wiedergab, weckten in mir ein tödliches Grauen, das umso grausiger war, als ich nicht enträtseln konnte, weshalb diese Bilder mich so schauerlich berührten; so lebhaft sie mir auch vor Augen stehen –

ich würde mich vergeblich bemühen, mehr von ihnen wiederzugeben als eben möglich ist, mit Worten flüchtig anzudeuten.

Durch die übertriebene Einfachheit, ja Nacktheit seiner Bilder fesselte er – erzwang er die Aufmerksamkeit.

Wenn je ein Sterblicher vermochte, eine Idee zu malen, so war es Roderick Usher.

Mich wenigstens überwältigte – unter den damals obwaltenden Umständen – bei den reinen Abstraktionen, die der Hypochonder wagte auf die Leinwand zu werfen –, mich überwältigte eine ganz unerhörte Ehrfurcht, von der ich nicht einen Schatten hatte empfinden können bei der Betrachtung der sicherlich glühenden, aber doch zu körperlichen Träume Füßlis.

Eines der phantastischen Gemälde meines Freundes, ein Bild, das nicht so streng abstrakt war, sei hier schattenhaft nachgezeichnet – so gut es Worte eben können.

Es war ein kleines Bild und zeigte das Innere eines ungeheuer langen rechtwinkligen Gewölbes oder Tunnels mit niederen, glatten weißen Mauern, die sich ohne jede Teilung schmucklos und endlos hinzogen.

Durch gewisse feine Andeutungen in der Zeichnung des Ganzen wurde im Beschauer der Gedanke erweckt, dass dieser Schacht sehr, sehr tief unter der Erde lag.

No outlet was observed in any portion of its vast extent, and no torch, or other artificial source of light was discernible; yet a flood of intense rays rolled throughout, and bathed the whole in a ghastly and inappropriate splendour.

I have just spoken of that morbid condition of the auditory nerve which rendered all music intolerable to the sufferer, with the exception of certain effects of stringed instruments.

It was, perhaps, the narrow limits to which he thus confined himself upon the guitar, which gave birth, in great measure, to the fantastic character of the performances.

But the fervid facility of his impromptus could not be so accounted for.

They must have been, and were, in the notes, as well as in the words of his wild fantasias (for he not unfrequently accompanied himself with rhymed verbal improvisations), the result of that intense mental collectedness and concentration to which I have previously alluded as observable only in particular moments of the highest artificial excitement.

The words of one of these rhapsodies I have easily remembered.

I was, perhaps, the more forcibly impressed with it, as he gave it, because, in the under or mystic current of its meaning, I fancied that I perceived, and for the first time, a full consciousness on the part of Usher, of the tottering of his lofty reason upon her throne.

The verses, which were entitled "The Haunted Palace," ran very nearly, if not accurately, thus:

I.

Nirgends fand sich in dieser Höhle eine Öffnung, und keine Fackel noch andere künstliche Lichtquelle war wahrnehmbar – dennoch quoll durch das Ganze eine Flut intensiver Strahlen und tauchte alles in eine gespenstische und ganz unvermutete Helligkeit.

Ich habe vorhin schon von der krankhaften Überreizung der Gehörsnerven gesprochen, die dem Leidenden alle Musik unerträglich machte, ausgenommen die Klangwirkung gewisser Saiteninstrumente.

Vielleicht war es hauptsächlich diese Einschränkung, durch die er auf die Gitarre angewiesen war, die seinen Vorträgen solch phantastischen Charakter lieh.

Aber das erklärte noch nicht die feurige Lebendigkeit dieser Impromptus.

Sicherlich waren sie, sowohl was die Töne als was die Worte anbetraf (denn nicht selten begleitete er sein Spiel mit improvisierten Versgesängen), das Resultat jener intensiven geistigen Anspannung und Konzentration, von der ich schon früher erwähnte, dass sie nur in besonderen Momenten höchster künstlerischer Erregtheit bemerkbar war.

Die Worte einer dieser Rhapsodien sind mir noch gut in Erinnerung.

Sie machten wohl einen um so gewaltigeren Eindruck auf mich, als ich in ihrem mystischen Inhalt eine verborgene Andeutung zu entdecken glaubte, dass Usher ein klares Bewusstsein davon habe, wie sehr seine erhabene Vernunft ins Wanken geraten sei.

Die Verse, die betitelt waren ›Der verzauberte Palast‹, lauteten ungefähr – wenn nicht wörtlich – so:

I.

In the greenest of our valleys,
  By good angels tenanted,
Once a fair and stately palace--
  Radiant palace--reared its head.
In the monarch Thought's dominion--
  It stood there!
Never seraph spread a pinion
  Over fabric half so fair.

II.

Banners yellow, glorious, golden,
  On its roof did float and flow;
(This--all this--was in the olden
  Time long ago)
And every gentle air that dallied,
  In that sweet day,
Along the ramparts plumed and pallid,
  A winged odour went away.

III.

Wanderers in that happy valley
  Through two luminous windows saw
Spirits moving musically
  To a lute's well tuned law,
Round about a throne, where sitting
  (Porphyrogene!)
In state his glory well befitting,
  The ruler of the realm was seen.

IV.

And all with pearl and ruby glowing
  Was the fair palace door,
Through which came flowing, flowing, flowing
  And sparkling evermore,
A troop of Echoes whose sweet duty
  Was but to sing,
In voices of surpassing beauty,
  The wit and wisdom of their king.

V.

But evil things, in robes of sorrow,
  Assailed the monarch's high estate;
(Ah, let us mourn, for never morrow
  Shall dawn upon him, desolate!)
And, round about his home, the glory
  That blushed and bloomed
Is but a dim-remembered story,
  Of the old time entombed.

In der Täler grünstem Tale hat,
  von Engeln einst bewohnt,
Gleich des Himmels Kathedrale
  Golddurchstrahlt ein Schloss gethront.
Rings auf Erden diesem Schlosse
  Keines glich;
Herrschte dort mit reichem Trosse
  Der Gedanke – königlich.

II.

Gelber Fahnen Faltenschlagen
  Floß wie Sonnengold im Wind –
Ach, es war in alten Tagen,
  Die nun längst vergangen sind! –
Damals kosten süße Lüfte
  Lind den Ort,
Zogen als beschwingte Düfte
  Von des Schlosses Wällen fort.

III.

Wandrer in dem Tale schauten
  Durch der Fenster lichten Glanz,
Geister zu dem Sang der Lauten
  Schreiten in gemessenem Tanz
Um den Thron, auf dem erhaben,
  Marmorschön,
Würdig solcher Weihegaben
  War des Reiches Herr zu sehen.

IV.

Perlengleich, rubinenglutend
  War des stolzen Schlosses Tor,
Ihm entschwebten flutend, flutend
  Süße Echos, die im Chor,
Weithinklingend, froh besangen
  – Süße Pflicht! –
Ihres Königs hehres Prangen
  In der Weisheit Himmelslicht.

V.

Doch Dämonen, schwarze Sorgen,
  Stürzten roh des Königs Thron. –
Trauert, Freunde, denn kein Morgen
  Wird ein Schloss wie dies umloh'n!
Was da blühte, was da glühte
  – Herrlichkeit! –
Eine welke Märchenblüte
  Ist's aus längst begrabner Zeit.

VI.

And travellers now within that valley,
  Through the red-litten windows, see
Vast forms that move fantastically
  To a discordant melody;
While, like a rapid ghastly river,
  Through the pale door,
A hideous throng rush out forever,
  And laugh--but smile no more.

I well remember that suggestions arising from this ballad, led us into a train of thought wherein there became manifest an opinion of Usher's

which I mention not so much on account of its novelty (for other men* have thought thus,) as on account of the pertinacity with which he maintained it.

This opinion, in its general form, was that of the sentience of all vegetable things.

But, in his disordered fancy, the idea had assumed a more daring character, and trespassed, under certain conditions, upon the kingdom of inorganization.

I lack words to express the full extent, or the earnest abandon of his persuasion.

The belief, however, was connected (as I have previously hinted) with the gray stones of the home of his forefathers.

The conditions of the sentience had been here, he imagined, fulfilled in the method of collocation of these stones--in the order of their arrangement, as well as in that of the many fungi which overspread them, and of the decayed trees which stood around--above all, in the long undisturbed endurance of this arrangement, and in its reduplication in the still waters of the tarn.

VI.

Und durch glutenrote Fenster
  Werden heute Wandrer sehn
Ungeheure Wahngespenster
  Grauenhaft im Tanz sich drehn;
Aus dem Tor in wilden Wellen,
  Wie ein Meer,
Lachend ekle Geister quellen –
  Ach, sie lächeln niemals mehr!

Ich entsinne mich gut, daß diese Ballade uns auf ein Gespräch führte, in dem Usher eine seltsame Anschauung kundgab.

Ich erwähne diese Anschauung weniger darum, weil sie etwa besonders neu wäre (denn andere haben ähnliche Hypothesen aufgestellt), als wegen der Hartnäckigkeit, mit der Usher sie vertrat.

Seine Anschauung bestand in der Hauptsache darin, daß er den Pflanzen ein Empfindungsvermögen, eine Beseeltheit zuschrieb.

Doch hatte in seinem verwirrten Geist diese Vorstellung einen kühneren Charakter angenommen und setzte sich in gewissen Grenzen auch ins Reich des Anorganischen fort.

Es fehlen mir die Worte, um die ganze Ausdehnung dieser Idee, um die unbeirrte Hingabe meines Freundes an sie auszudrücken.

Dieser sein Glaube knüpfte sich (wie ich schon früher andeutete) eng an die grauen Quadern des Heims seiner Väter.

Die Vorbedingungen für solches Empfindungsvermögen waren hier, wie er sich einbildete, erfüllt in der Art der Anordnung der Steine, in dem sie zusammenhaltenden Bindemittel und ebenso auch in dem Pilzgeflecht, das sie überwucherte; ferner in den abgestorbenen Bäumen, die das Haus umgaben, und vor allem in dem nie gestörten, unveränderten Bestehen des Ganzen und in seiner Verdoppelung in

Its evidence--the evidence of the sentience--was to be seen, he said, (and I here started as he spoke,) in the gradual yet certain condensation of an atmosphere of their own about the waters and the walls.

The result was discoverable, he added, in that silent, yet importunate and terrible influence which for centuries had moulded the destinies of his family, and which made him what I now saw him--what he was.

Such opinions need no comment, and I will make none.

Our books--the books which, for years, had formed no small portion of the mental existence of the invalid--were, as might be supposed, in strict keeping with this character of phantasm.

We pored together over such works as the Ververt et Chartreuse of Gresset; the Belphegor of Machiavelli; the Heaven and Hell of Swedenborg; the Subterranean Voyage of Nicholas Klimm by Holberg; the Chiromancy of Robert Flud, of Jean D'Indagine, and of De la Chambre; the Journey into the Blue Distance of Tieck; and the City of the Sun by Campanella.

One favourite volume was a small octavo edition of the Directorium Inquisitorum, by the Dominican Eymeric de Gironne; and there were passages in Pomponius Mela, about the old African Satyrs and OEgipans, over which Usher would sit dreaming for hours.

His chief delight, however, was found in

den stillen Wassern des Teiches.

Der Beweis – der Beweis dieser Beseeltheit – sei, so sagte er, zu erblicken (und als er das aussprach, schrak ich zusammen) in der hier ganz allmählichen, jedoch unablässig fortschreitenden Verdichtung der Atmosphäre – in dem eigentümlichen Dunstkreis, der Wasser und Wälle umgab.

Die Wirkung dieser Erscheinung, fügte er hinzu, sei der lautlos und grässlich zunehmende vernichtende Einfluss, den sie seit Jahrhunderten auf das Geschick seiner Familie ausgeübt habe; sie habe ihn zu dem gemacht, als den ich ihn jetzt erblicke – zu dem, was er nun sei.

– Solche Anschauungen bedürfen keines Kommentars, und ich füge ihnen daher nichts hinzu.

Unsere Bücher – die Bücher, die jahrelang des Kranken hauptsächliche Geistesnahrung gebildet hatten – entsprachen, wie vermutet werden konnte, diesem phantastischen Charakter.

Wir grübelten gemeinsam über solchen Werken wie ›Ververt et Chartreuse‹ von Grasset, ›Belphegor‹ von Macchiavelli, ›Himmel und Hölle‹ von Swedenborg, ›Die unterirdische Reise des Nicolaus Klimm‹ von Holberg, die Chiromantie von Robert Flud, von Jean d'Indaginé und von de la Chambre; brüteten über der ›Reise ins Blaue‹ von Tieck und der ›Stadt der Sonne‹ von Campanella.

Ein Lieblingsbuch war eine kleine Oktav-Ausgabe des ›Directorium Inquisitorium‹ des Dominikaners Emmerich von Gironne, und es gab Stellen in ›Pomponius Mela‹ über die alten afrikanischen Satyrn und Ögipans, vor denen Usher stundenlang träumend sitzen konnte.

Sein Hauptentzücken jedoch bildete das

the perusal of an exceedingly rare and curious book in quarto Gothic--the manual of a forgotten church--the Vigiliae Mortuorum Secundum Chorum Ecclesiae Maguntinae.

I could not help thinking of the wild ritual of this work, and of its probable influence upon the hypochondriac, when, one evening, having informed me abruptly that the lady Madeline was no more, he stated his intention of preserving her corpse for a fortnight, (previously to its final interment), in one of the numerous vaults within the main walls of the building.

The worldly reason, however, assigned for this singular proceeding, was one which I did not feel at liberty to dispute.

The brother had been led to his resolution (so he told me) by consideration of the unusual character of the malady of the deceased, of certain obtrusive and eager inquiries on the part of her medical men, and of the remote and exposed situation of the burial-ground of the family.

I will not deny that when I called to mind the sinister countenance of the person whom I met upon the staircase, on the day of my arrival at the house, I had no desire to oppose what I regarded as at best but a harmless, and by no means an unnatural, precaution.

At the request of Usher, I personally aided him in the arrangements for the temporary entombment.

The body having been encoffined, we two alone bore it to its rest.

The vault in which we placed it (and which had been so long unopened that

Studium eines sehr seltenen und seltsamen Buches in gotischem Quartformat – einem Handbuch einer vergessenen Kirche –, des ›Vigiliae Mortuorum secundum Chorum Ecclesiae Maguntinae‹.

Ich konnte nicht anders, als an das seltsame Ritual dieses Werkes und seinen wahrscheinlichen Einfluss auf den Schwermütigen denken, als er eines Abends, nachdem er mir kurz mitgeteilt hatte, dass Lady Magdalen nicht mehr sei, seine Absicht äußerte, den Leichnam vor seiner endgültigen Beerdigung in einer der zahlreichen Grüfte innerhalb der Grundmauern des Gebäudes aufzubewahren.

Die rein äußere Ursache, die er für dieses Vorgehen angab, war solcher Art, dass ich mich nicht aufgelegt fühlte, darüber zu diskutieren.

Er, der Bruder, war (wie er mir sagte) zu diesem Entschluss gekommen infolge des ungewöhnlichen Charakters der Krankheit der Dahingeschiedenen, infolge gewisser eifriger und eindringlicher Fragen ihres Arztes und infolge der abgelegenen und einsamen Lage des Begräbnisplatzes der Familie.

Ich will nicht leugnen, dass, wenn ich mir das finstere Gesicht des Mannes ins Gedächtnis rief, dem ich am Tage meiner Ankunft auf der Treppe begegnete – dass ich dann kein Verlangen hatte, einer Sache zu widersprechen, die ich nur als eine harmlose und keineswegs unnatürliche Vorsichtsmaßregel ansah.

Auf Bitten Ushers half ich ihm bei den Vorkehrungen für die vorläufige Bestattung.

Nachdem der Körper eingesargt worden war, trugen wir ihn beide ganz allein zu seiner Ruhestätte.

Die Gruft, in der wir ihn beisetzten, war so lange nicht geöffnet worden, dass

our torches, half smothered in its oppressive atmosphere, gave us little opportunity for investigation)

was small, damp, and entirely without means of admission for light; lying, at great depth, immediately beneath that portion of the building in which was my own sleeping apartment.

It had been used, apparently, in remote feudal times, for the worst purposes of a donjon-keep, and, in later days, as a place of deposit for powder, or some other highly combustible substance, as a portion of its floor, and the whole interior of a long archway through which we reached it, were carefully sheathed with copper.

The door, of massive iron, had been, also, similarly protected.

Its immense weight caused an unusually sharp grating sound, as it moved upon its hinges.

Having deposited our mournful burden upon tressels within this region of horror, we partially turned aside the yet unscrewed lid of the coffin, and looked upon the face of the tenant.

A striking similitude between the brother and sister now first arrested my attention; and Usher, divining, perhaps, my thoughts, murmured out some few words from which I learned that the deceased and himself had been twins, and that sympathies of a scarcely intelligible nature had always existed between them.

Our glances, however, rested not long upon the dead--for we could not regard her unawed.

unsere Fackeln in der drückenden Atmosphäre fast erstickten und uns nur wenig gestatteten, Umschau zu halten.

Die Gruft war eng, dumpfig und ohne jegliche Öffnung, die Licht hätte einlassen können; sie lag in beträchtlicher Tiefe, genau unter dem Teil des Hauses, in dem sich mein eigenes Schlafgemach befand.

Augenscheinlich hatte sie in früheren Zeiten der Feudalherrschaft als Burgverlies übelste Verwendung gefunden und hatte später als Lagerraum für Pulver oder sonst einen leicht entzündlichen Stoff gedient, denn ein Teil ihres Fußbodens sowie das ganze Innere eines langen Bogenganges, von dem aus wir das Gewölbe erreichten, war sorgfältig mit Kupfer bekleidet.

Die Tür aus massivem Eisen hatte ähnliche Schutzvorrichtungen.

Ihr ungeheures Gewicht brachte einen ungewöhnlich scharfen kreischenden Laut hervor, als sie sich schwerfällig in den Angeln drehte.

Nachdem wir unsere traurige Bürde an diesem Ort des Grauens auf ein vorbereitetes Gestell niedergesetzt hatten, schoben wir den noch lose aufliegenden Deckel des Sarges ein wenig zur Seite und blickten in das Antlitz der Ruhenden.

Eine verblüffende Ähnlichkeit zwischen Bruder und Schwester fesselte jetzt zum erstenmal meine Aufmerksamkeit, und Usher, der vielleicht meine Gedanken erriet, murmelte ein paar Worte, denen ich entnahm, dass die Verstorbene und er Zwillinge gewesen waren, und dass Sympathien ganz ungewöhnlicher Natur stets zwischen ihnen bestanden hatten.

Unsere Blicke ruhten jedoch nicht lange auf der Toten – denn wir konnten sie nicht ohne Ergriffenheit und Grausen betrachten.

The disease which had thus entombed the lady in the maturity of youth, had left, as usual in all maladies of a strictly cataleptical character, the mockery of a faint blush upon the bosom and the face, and that suspiciously lingering smile upon the lip which is so terrible in death.

We replaced and screwed down the lid, and, having secured the door of iron, made our way, with toil, into the scarcely less gloomy apartments of the upper portion of the house.

And now, some days of bitter grief having elapsed, an observable change came over the features of the mental disorder of my friend.

His ordinary manner had vanished.

His ordinary occupations were neglected or forgotten.

He roamed from chamber to chamber with hurried, unequal, and objectless step.

The pallor of his countenance had assumed, if possible, a more ghastly hue--but the luminousness of his eye had utterly gone out.

The once occasional huskiness of his tone was heard no more; and a tremulous quaver, as if of extreme terror, habitually characterized his utterance.

There were times, indeed, when I thought his unceasingly agitated mind was labouring with some oppressive secret, to divulge which he struggled for the necessary courage.

At times, again, I was obliged to resolve all into the mere inexplicable vagaries of madness, for I beheld him gazing upon vacancy for long hours, in an attitude of

---

Das Leiden, das die Lady so in der Blüte der Jugend ins Grab gebracht, hatte – wie es bei Erkrankungen ausgesprochen kataleptischer Art gewöhnlich der Fall ist – auf Hals und Antlitz so etwas wie eine schwache Röte zurückgelassen und den Lippen ein argwöhnisch lauerndes Lächeln gegeben, das so schrecklich ist bei Toten.

Wir setzten den Deckel wieder auf, schraubten ihn fest, und nachdem wir die Eisentüre wieder verschlossen hatten, nahmen wir mit Mühe unsern Weg hinauf in die kaum weniger düstern Räumlichkeiten des oberen Stockwerkes.

Und jetzt, nachdem einige Tage bittersten Kummers vergangen waren, trat in der Geistesverwirrung meines Freundes eine merkliche Änderung ein.

Sein ganzes Wesen wurde ein anderes.

Seine gewöhnlichen Beschäftigungen wurden vernachlässigt oder vergessen.

Er schweifte von Zimmer zu Zimmer mit eiligem, unsicherem und ziellosem Schritt.

Die Blässe seines Gesichts war womöglich noch gespenstischer geworden – aber der feurige Glanz seiner Augen war ganz erloschen.

Die gelegentliche Heiserkeit seiner Stimme war nicht mehr zu hören, und ein Zittern und Schwanken, wie von namenlosem Entsetzen, durchbebte gewöhnlich seine Worte.

Es gab in der Tat Zeiten, wo ich vermeinte, sein unablässig arbeitender Geist kämpfe mit irgendeinem drückenden Geheimnis, zu dessen Bekenntnis er nicht den Mut finden könne.

Zu andern Zeiten wieder war ich gezwungen, alles lediglich als Äußerungen seiner seltsamen Krankheit aufzufassen, denn ich sah, wie er

the profoundest attention, as if listening to some imaginary sound.

It was no wonder that his condition terrified--that it infected me.

I felt creeping upon me, by slow yet certain degrees, the wild influences of his own fantastic yet impressive superstitions.

It was, especially, upon retiring to bed late in the night of the seventh or eighth day after the placing of the lady Madeline within the donjon, that I experienced the full power of such feelings.

Sleep came not near my couch--while the hours waned and waned away.

I struggled to reason off the nervousness which had dominion over me.

I endeavoured to believe that much, if not all of what I felt, was due to the bewildering influence of the gloomy furniture of the room--of the dark and tattered draperies, which, tortured into motion by the breath of a rising tempest, swayed fitfully to and fro upon the walls, and rustled uneasily about the decorations of the bed.

But my efforts were fruitless.

An irrepressible tremor gradually pervaded my frame; and, at length, there sat upon my very heart an incubus of utterly causeless alarm.

Shaking this off with a gasp and a struggle, I uplifted myself upon the pillows, and, peering earnestly within the intense darkness of the chamber, hearkened--I know not why, except that an instinctive spirit prompted me--to

stundenlang ins Leere starrte – und zwar mit dem Ausdruck tiefster Aufmerksamkeit, als lauschte er irgendeinem eingebildeten Geräusch.

Es war kein Wunder, dass sein Zustand mich erschreckte, mich ansteckte.

Ich fühlte, wie sich ganz allmählich, doch unablässig seine seltsamen Wahnvorstellungen, die er mir niemals mitteilte, in mich hineinfraßen.

Es war besonders in der Nacht des siebenten oder achten Tages nach der Bestattung der Lady Magdalen in der Gruft, als ich mich sehr spät zum Schlafen zurückgezogen hatte, dass ich die volle Gewalt dieser Empfindungen erfuhr.

Kein Schlaf nahte sich meinem Lager, während die Stunden träge dahinkrochen.

Ich bemühte mich, der Nervosität, die mich ergriffen hatte, Herr zu werden.

Ich suchte mich zu überzeugen, dass an vielem – wenn nicht an allem –, was ich fühlte, die unheimliche Einrichtung des Gemachs schuld sei; denn es war unheimlich, wie die dunklen und zerschlissenen Wandteppiche, vom Atem eines nahenden Sturmes bewegt, stoßweise auf- und niederschwankten und gegen die Verzierungen des Bettes raschelten.

Aber meine Anstrengungen waren fruchtlos.

Ein nicht abzuschüttelndes Grauen durchbebte meinen Körper, und schließlich hockte auf meinem Herzen ein Alp – ein furchtbarstes Entsetzen.

Mit einem tiefen Atemzug rang ich mich frei aus diesem Bann und setzte mich im Bette auf, ich spähte angestrengt in das undurchdringliche Dunkel des Zimmers und lauschte – wie getrieben von seltsamen instinktiven Ahnungen – auf

certain low and indefinite sounds which came, through the pauses of the storm, at long intervals, I knew not whence.

Overpowered by an intense sentiment of horror, unaccountable yet unendurable, I threw on my clothes with haste (for I felt that I should sleep no more during the night,) and endeavoured to arouse myself from the pitiable condition into which I had fallen, by pacing rapidly to and fro through the apartment.

I had taken but few turns in this manner, when a light step on an adjoining staircase arrested my attention.

I presently recognized it as that of Usher.

In an instant afterwards he rapped, with a gentle touch, at my door, and entered, bearing a lamp.

His countenance was, as usual, cadaverously wan--but, moreover, there was a species of mad hilarity in his eyes--an evidently restrained hysteria in his whole demeanour.

His air appalled me--but anything was preferable to the solitude which I had so long endured, and I even welcomed his presence as a relief.

"And you have not seen it?"

he said abruptly, after having stared about him for some moments in silence--"you have not then seen it?--

but, stay! you shall."

Thus speaking, and having carefully shaded his lamp, he hurried to one of the casements, and threw it freely open to the storm.

gewisse dumpfe, unbestimmbare Laute, die, wenn der Sturm schwieg, in langen Zwischenräumen von irgendwoher zu mir drangen.

Überwältigt von unbeschreiblichem Entsetzen, das mir ebenso unerträglich wie unerklärlich schien, warf ich mich hastig in die Kleider (denn ich fühlte, dass ich in dieser Nacht doch keinen Schlaf mehr finden würde) und versuchte, mich aus meinem jammervollen Zustand aufzuraffen, indem ich eilig im Zimmer auf- und abwandelte.

Ich war erst ein paarmal so hin und her gegangen, als ein leichter Tritt auf der benachbarten Treppe meine Aufmerksamkeit erregte.

Ich erkannte sogleich Ushers Schritt.

Einen Augenblick später klopfte er leise an meine Tür und trat mit einer Lampe in der Hand ein.

Sein Gesicht war wie immer leichenhaft blass – aber schrecklicher war der Ausdruck seiner Augen: wie eine irrsinnige Heiterkeit flammte es aus ihnen – sein ganzes Gebaren zeigte eine mühsam gebändigte hysterische Aufregung.

Sein Ausdruck entsetzte mich – doch alles schien erträglicher als diese fürchterliche Einsamkeit, und ich begrüßte sein Kommen wie eine Erlösung.

"Und du hast es nicht gesehen?"

sagte er unvermittelt, nachdem er einige Augenblicke schweigend um sich geblickt hatte. "Du hast es also nicht gesehen?

– Doch halt, du sollst!"

Mit diesen Worten beschattete er sorgsam seine Lampe und lief dann an eins der Fenster, das er dem Sturm weit öffnete.

The impetuous fury of the entering gust nearly lifted us from our feet.

It was, indeed, a tempestuous yet sternly beautiful night, and one wildly singular in its terror and its beauty.

A whirlwind had apparently collected its force in our vicinity; for there were frequent and violent alterations in the direction of the wind;

and the exceeding density of the clouds (which hung so low as to press upon the turrets of the house) did not prevent our perceiving the lifelike velocity with which they flew careering from all points against each other, without passing away into the distance.

I say that even their exceeding density did not prevent our perceiving this--yet we had no glimpse of the moon or stars-- nor was there any flashing forth of the lightning.

But the under surfaces of the huge masses of agitated vapor, as well as all terrestrial objects immediately around us, were glowing in the unnatural light of a faintly luminous and distinctly visible gaseous exhalation which hung about and enshrouded the mansion.

"You must not--you shall not behold this!"

said I, shudderingly, to Usher, as I led him, with a gentle violence, from the window to a seat.

"These appearances, which bewilder you, are merely electrical phenomena not uncommon--or it may be that they have their ghastly origin in the rank miasma of the tarn.

Let us close this casement;--the air is

Die ungeheure Wut des hereinstürmenden Orkans hob uns fast vom Boden empor.

Es war wirklich eine sturmrasende, aber doch sehr schöne Nacht –, eine Nacht, die grausig seltsam war in Schrecken und in Pracht.

Ganz in unserer Nachbarschaft musste sich ein Wirbelwind erhoben haben, denn die Windstöße änderten häufig ihre Richtung.

Die ungewöhnliche Dichtigkeit der Wolken, die so tief hingen, als lasteten sie auf den Türmen des Hauses, verhinderte nicht die Wahrnehmung, dass sie wie mit bewusster Hast aus allen Richtungen herbeijagten und ineinanderstürzten – ohne aber weiterzuziehen.

Ich sage: selbst ihre ungewöhnliche Dichtigkeit verhinderte uns nicht, dies wahrzunehmen – dennoch erblickten wir keinen Schimmer vom Mond oder von den Sternen – ebensowenig aber einen Blitzstrahl.

Doch die unteren Flächen der jagenden Wolkenmassen und alle umgebenden Dinge draußen im Freien glühten im unnatürlichen Licht eines schwach leuchtenden und deutlich sichtbaren gasartigen Dunstes, der das Haus umgab und einhüllte.

"Du darfst – du sollst das nicht sehen!"

sagte ich schaudernd zu Usher, als ich ihn mit sanfter Gewalt vom Fenster fort zu einem Sessel führte.

"Diese Erscheinungen, die dich erschrecken, sind nichts Ungewöhnliches; es sind elektrische Ausstrahlungen – vielleicht auch verdanken sie ihr gespenstisches Dasein der schwülen Ausdünstung des Teiches.

Wir wollen das Fenster schließen; die

chilling and dangerous to your frame. Here is one of your favourite romances. I will read, and you shall listen;--and so we will pass away this terrible night together."

The antique volume which I had taken up was the "Mad Trist" of Sir Launcelot Canning; but I had called it a favourite of Usher's more in sad jest than in earnest; for, in truth, there is little in its uncouth and unimaginative prolixity which could have had interest for the lofty and spiritual ideality of my friend.

It was, however, the only book immediately at hand; and I indulged a vague hope that the excitement which now agitated the hypochondriac, might find relief (for the history of mental disorder is full of similar anomalies) even in the extremeness of the folly which I should read.

Could I have judged, indeed, by the wild overstrained air of vivacity with which he hearkened, or apparently hearkened, to the words of the tale, I might well have congratulated myself upon the success of my design.

I had arrived at that well-known portion of the story where Ethelred, the hero of the Trist, having sought in vain for peaceable admission into the dwelling of the hermit, proceeds to make good an entrance by force.

Here, it will be remembered, the words of the narrative run thus:

"And Ethelred, who was by nature of a doughty heart, and who was now mighty withal, on account of the powerfulness of the wine which he had drunken, waited no longer to hold parley with the hermit, who, in sooth, was of an obstinate and maliceful turn,

Luft ist kühl und dir sehr unzuträglich. – Hier ist eines deiner Lieblingsbücher. Ich will vorlesen und du sollst zuhören, und so wollen wir diese fürchterliche Nacht zusammen verbringen."

Der alte Band, den ich zur Hand genommen hatte, war der ›Mad Trist‹ von Sir Launcelot Canning, aber ich hatte ihn mehr in traurigem Scherz als im Ernst Ushers Lieblingsbuch genannt; denn in Wahrheit ist in seiner ungefügten und phantasielosen Weitschweifigkeit wenig, was für den scharfsinnigen und idealen Geist meines Freundes von Interesse sein konnte.

Es war jedoch das einzige Buch, das ich zur Hand hatte, und ich nährte eine schwache Hoffnung, der aufgeregte Zustand des Hypochonders möge Beruhigung finden (denn die Geschichte geistiger Zerrüttung weist solche Widersprüche auf) in den tollen Übertriebenheiten, die ich lesen wollte.

Hätte ich wirklich nach der gespannten, ja leidenschaftlichen Aufmerksamkeit schließen dürfen, mit der er mir zuhörte – oder zuzuhören schien –, so hätte ich mir zu dem Erfolg meines Vorhabens Glück wünschen dürfen.

Ich war in der Erzählung bei der allbekannten Stelle angelangt, wo Ethelred, der Held des ›Trist‹, nachdem er vergeblich friedlichen Einlass in die Hütte des Klausners zu bekommen versucht hatte, sich anschickt, den Eintritt durch Gewalt zu erzwingen.

Hier lautet der Text, wie man sich erinnern wird, so:

"Und Ethelred, der von Natur ein mannhaft Herz hatte und der nun, nachdem er den kräftigen Wein getrunken, sich unermesslich stark fühlte, begnügte sich nicht länger, mit dem Klausner Zwiesprach zu halten, der wirklich voll Trotz und Bosheit war,

but, feeling the rain upon his shoulders, and fearing the rising of the tempest, uplifted his mace outright, and, with blows, made quickly room in the plankings of the door for his gauntleted hand; and now pulling therewith sturdily, he so cracked, and ripped, and tore all asunder, that the noise of the dry and hollow-sounding wood alarmed and reverberated throughout the forest."

At the termination of this sentence I started, and for a moment, paused; for it appeared to me (although I at once concluded that my excited fancy had deceived me)--it appeared to me that, from some very remote portion of the mansion, there came, indistinctly, to my ears, what might have been, in its exact similarity of character, the echo (but a stifled and dull one certainly) of the very cracking and ripping sound which Sir Launcelot had so particularly described.

It was, beyond doubt, the coincidence alone which had arrested my attention; for, amid the rattling of the sashes of the casements, and the ordinary commingled noises of the still increasing storm, the sound, in itself, had nothing, surely, which should have interested or disturbed me.

I continued the story:

"But the good champion Ethelred, now entering within the door, was sore enraged and amazed to perceive no signal of the maliceful hermit; but, in the stead thereof, a dragon of a scaly and prodigious demeanour, and of a fiery tongue, which sate in guard before a palace of gold, with a floor of silver;

and upon the wall there hung a shield of shining brass with this legend enwritten-- Who entereth herein, a

---

sondern da er auf seinen Schultern schon den Regen fühlte und den herannahenden Sturm fürchtete, schwang er seinen Streitkolben hoch hinaus und schaffte in den Planken der Tür schnell Raum für seine behandschuhte Hand; und nun fasste er derb zu und zerkrachte und zerbrach – und riss alles zusammen, dass der Lärm des dürren, dumpf krachenden Holzes durch den ganzen Wald schallte und widerhallte."

Bei Beendigung dieses Satzes fuhr ich auf und hielt mit Lesen inne, denn es schien mir so (obwohl ich sofort überlegte, dass meine erhitzte Phantasie mich getäuscht haben müsse), als kämen aus einem ganz entlegenen Teile des Hauses Geräusche her, die ein vollkommenes sehr fernes Echo hätten sein können von jenem Krachen und Bersten, das Sir Launcelot so charakteristisch beschrieben hatte.

Zweifellos war es nur das Zusammentreffen irgendeines Geräusches mit meinen Worten, das meine Aufmerksamkeit gefesselt hatte. Denn inmitten des Rüttelns der Fensterläden und der vielfältigen Lärmlaute des anwachsenden Sturmes hatte der Laut an sich sicherlich nichts, was mich interessiert oder gestört haben könnte.

Ich fuhr in der Erzählung fort:

"Aber als der werte Held Ethelred jetzt in die Türe trat, geriet er bald in Wut und Bestürzung, kein Zeichen des boshaften Klausners zu bemerken, sondern statt seiner ein ungeheurer schuppenrasselnder Drachen mit feuriger Zunge, der als Hüter vor einem goldenen Palast mit silbernem Fußboden ruhte.

Und an der Mauer hing ein Schild aus schimmerndem Stahl mit der Inschrift: ›Wer hier herein will dringen, den

conquerer hath bin; Who slayeth the dragon, the shield he shall win;

and Ethelred uplifted his mace, and struck upon the head of the dragon, which fell before him, and gave up his pesty breath, with a shriek so horrid and harsh, and withal so piercing, that Ethelred had fain to close his ears with his hands against the dreadful noise of it, the like whereof was never before heard."

Here again I paused abruptly, and now with a feeling of wild amazement--for there could be no doubt whatever that, in this instance, I did actually hear (although from what direction it proceeded I found it impossible to say)

a low and apparently distant, but harsh, protracted, and most unusual screaming or grating sound--the exact counterpart of what my fancy had already conjured up for the dragon's unnatural shriek as described by the romancer.

Oppressed, as I certainly was, upon the occurrence of the second and most extraordinary coincidence, by a thousand conflicting sensations, in which wonder and extreme terror were predominant, I still retained sufficient presence of mind to avoid exciting, by any observation, the sensitive nervousness of my companion.

I was by no means certain that he had noticed the sounds in question; although, assuredly, a strange alteration had, during the last few minutes, taken place in his demeanour.

From a position fronting my own, he had gradually brought round his chair, so as to sit with his face to the door of the chamber; and thus I could but partially perceive his features, although I saw that his lips trembled as if he were

Drachen muss er bezwingen; Ein Held wird er sein, den Schild sich erringen.‹

Und Ethelred schwang seinen Streitkolben und schmetterte ihn auf den Schädel des Drachen, der zusammenbrach und seinen üblen Odem aufgab, und dieses mit einem so grässlichen und schrillen und durchdringenden Schrei, dass Ethelred sich gern die Ohren zugehalten hätte vor dem schrecklichen Laut, desgleichen hiervor niemanden erhört gewesen war."

Hier hielt ich wieder bestürzt inne – und diesmal mit schauderndem Entsetzen –, denn es konnte kein Zweifel sein, dass ich in diesem Augenblick (wennschon es mir unmöglich war, anzugeben, aus welcher Richtung)

einen dumpfen und offenbar entfernten, aber schrillen, langgezogenen, kreischenden Laut vernommen hatte – das vollkommene Gegenstück zu dem unnatürlichen Aufschrei des Drachen, wie der Dichter ihn beschrieb.

Obwohl ich durch dies zweite und höchst seltsame Zusammentreffen erschreckt war und tausend widerstreitende Empfindungen, in denen Erstaunen und äußerstes Entsetzen vorherrschten, mich bestürmten, hatte ich dennoch Geistesgegenwart genug, nicht etwa durch eine diesbezügliche Bemerkung die Nervosität meines Gefährten noch zu steigern.

Ich war keineswegs sicher, dass er die in Frage stehenden Laute vernommen hatte, obgleich allerdings während der letzten Minuten eine sonderbare Veränderung mit ihm vorgegangen war.

Anfänglich hatte er mir gegenüber gesessen, so dass ich ihm voll ins Gesicht sehen konnte; nach und nach aber hatte er seinen Stuhl so herumgedreht, dass er nun mit dem Gesicht zur Türe schaute.

murmuring inaudibly.

His head had dropped upon his breast--yet I knew that he was not asleep, from the wide and rigid opening of the eye as I caught a glance of it in profile.

The motion of his body, too, was at variance with this idea--for he rocked from side to side with a gentle yet constant and uniform sway.

Having rapidly taken notice of all this, I resumed the narrative of Sir Launcelot, which thus proceeded:

"And now, the champion, having escaped from the terrible fury of the dragon, bethinking himself of the brazen shield, and of the breaking up of the enchantment which was upon it, removed the carcass from out of the way before him, and approached valorously over the silver pavement of the castle to where the shield was upon the wall;

which in sooth tarried not for his full coming, but fell down at his feet upon the silver floor, with a mighty great and terrible ringing sound."

No sooner had these syllables passed my lips, than--as if a shield of brass had indeed, at the moment, fallen heavily upon a floor of silver--I became aware of a distinct, hollow, metallic, and clangorous, yet apparently muffled reverberation.

Completely unnerved, I leaped to my feet; but the measured rocking movement of Usher was undisturbed.

I rushed to the chair in which he sat.

His eyes were bent fixedly before him, and throughout his whole countenance there reigned a stony rigidity.

But, as I placed my hand upon his shoulder, there came a strong shudder

Ich konnte daher seine Züge nur teilweise erblicken, doch sah ich, dass seine Lippen zitterten, als flüstere er leise vor sich hin.

Der Kopf war ihm auf die Brust gesunken, aber ich wusste, dass er nicht schlief, denn sein Profil zeigte mir seine weit und starr geöffneten Augen, und sein Körper bewegte sich unausgesetzt sanft und einförmig hin und her.

Dies alles hatte ich mit raschem Blick erfasst und nahm nun die Erzählung Sir Launcelots wieder auf:

"Und nun, da der Held der schrecklichen Wut des Drachen entronnen war und sich des stählernen Schildes erinnerte, dessen Zauber nun gebrochen, räumte er den Kadaver beiseite und schritt über das silberne Pflaster kühn hin zu dem Schild an der Wand.

Der aber wartete nicht, bis er herangekommen war, sondern stürzte zu seinen Füßen auf den Silberboden nieder, mit gewaltig schmetterndem, furchtbar dröhnendem Getöse."

Kaum hatten meine Lippen diese Worte gesprochen, da vernahm ich – als sei in der Tat ein eherner Schild schwer auf einen silbernen Boden gestürzt – deutlich, aber gedämpft, einen metallisch dröhnenden Widerhall.

Gänzlich entnervt sprang ich auf die Füße, aber die taktmäßige Schaukelbewegung Ushers dauerte fort.

Ich stürzte zu dem Stuhl, in dem er saß.

Sein Blick war stier geradeaus gerichtet, und sein Antlitz schien wie zu Stein erstarrt.

Aber als ich die Hand auf seine Schulter legte, befiel ein heftiges Zittern seine

over his whole person; a sickly smile quivered about his lips; and I saw that he spoke in a low, hurried, and gibbering murmur, as if unconscious of my presence.

Bending closely over him, I at length drank in the hideous import of his words.

"Not hear it?

- yes, I hear it, and have heard it.

Long -- long -- long -- many minutes, many hours, many days, have I heard it-- yet I dared not--oh, pity me, miserable wretch that I am!

--I dared not--I dared not speak!

We have put her living in the tomb!

Said I not that my senses were acute?

I now tell you that I heard her first feeble movements in the hollow coffin.

I heard them--many, many days ago--yet I dared not--I dared not speak!

And now -- to-night -- Ethelred--ha! ha!

--the breaking of the hermit's door, and the death-cry of the dragon, and the clangour of the shield!

--say, rather, the rending of her coffin, and the grating of the iron hinges of her prison, and her struggles within the coppered archway of the vault!

Oh whither shall I fly?

Will she not be here anon?

Is she not hurrying to upbraid me for my haste?

Have I not heard her footsteps on the stair?

ganze Gestalt; ein krankes Lächeln zuckte um seinen Mund, und ich sah, dass er leise hastend und stotternd vor sich hin murmelte, so, als wisse er nichts von meiner Anwesenheit.

Mich tief zu ihm hinabbeugend, trank ich schließlich den scheußlichen Sinn seiner Worte ein:

"Es nicht hören?

– Oh, ich höre es wohl und habe es gehört.

Lange – lange – lange – viele Minuten, viele Stunden, viele Tage habe ich es gehört – aber ich wagte nicht – oh, bedaure mich – elender Schurke, der ich bin!

– Ich wagte nicht, ich wagte nicht zu reden!

Wir haben sie lebendig ins Grab gelegt!

Sagte ich nicht, meine Sinne seien scharf?

Ich sage dir jetzt, dass ich ihre ersten schwachen Bewegungen im dumpfen Sarge hörte.

Ich hörte sie – vor vielen, vielen Tagen schon – dennoch wagte ich nicht – ich wagte nicht zu reden!

– Und jetzt – heute Nacht – Ethelred – ha! ha!

– Das Aufbrechen der Tür des Klausners, und der Todesschrei des Drachen, und das Dröhnen des Schildes!

– Sage lieber: das Zerbersten ihres Sarges, und das Kreischen der eisernen Angeln ihres Gefängnisses, und ihr qualvolles Vorwärtskämpfen durch den kupfernen Bogengang des Gewölbes.

Oh, wohin soll ich fliehen?

Wird sie nicht gleich hier sein?

Wird sie nicht eilen, um mir meine Eile vorzuwerfen?

Hörte ich nicht schon ihren Tritt auf der Treppe?

Do I not distinguish that heavy and horrible beating of her heart?

Madman!"

here he sprang furiously to his feet, and shrieked out his syllables, as if in the effort he were giving up his soul--"Madman!

I tell you that she now stands without the door!"

As if in the superhuman energy of his utterance there had been found the potency of a spell--the huge antique panels to which the speaker pointed, threw slowly back, upon the instant, their ponderous and ebony jaws.

It was the work of the rushing gust--but then without those doors there DID stand the lofty and enshrouded figure of the lady Madeline of Usher.

There was blood upon her white robes, and the evidence of some bitter struggle upon every portion of her emaciated frame.

For a moment she remained trembling and reeling to and fro upon the threshold,--then, with a low moaning cry, fell heavily inward upon the person of her brother, and in her violent and now final death-agonies, bore him to the floor a corpse, and a victim to the terrors he had anticipated.

From that chamber, and from that mansion, I fled aghast.

The storm was still abroad in all its wrath as I found myself crossing the old causeway.

Suddenly there shot along the path a wild light, and I turned to see whence a gleam so unusual could have issued; for the vast house and its shadows were alone behind me.

Kann ich nicht schon das schwere und schreckliche Schlagen ihres Herzens vernehmen?

Wahnsinniger!"

– hier sprang er wie rasend auf und kreischte, als wolle er mit diesen Worten seine Seele hinausbrüllen –
"Wahnsinniger!

Ich sage dir, dass sie jetzt draußen vor der Türe steht!"

Als läge in der übermenschlichen Kraft dieses Ausrufes die Macht eines Zaubers – so rissen jetzt die riesigen alten Türflügel, auf die der Sprecher hinzeigte, ihre gewaltigen ebenholzenen Kinnladen auf.

Es war das Werk des rasenden Sturmes – aber siehe – draußen vor der Türe stand leibhaftig die hohe, ins Leichentuch gehüllte Gestalt der Lady Magdalen Usher.

Es war Blut auf ihrer weißen Gewandung, und die Spuren eines erbitterten Kampfes waren überall an ihrem abgezehrten Körper zu erkennen.

Einen Augenblick blieb sie zitternd und taumelnd auf der Schwelle stehen – dann fiel sie mit einem leisen schmerzlichen Aufschrei ins Zimmer auf den Körper ihres Bruders – und in ihrem heftigen und nun endgültigen Todeskampf riss sie ihn tot zu Boden – ein Opfer der Schrecken, die er vorausempfunden hatte.

Wie verfolgt entfloh ich aus diesem Gemach und diesem Hause.

Draußen tobte das Unwetter in unverminderter Heftigkeit, als ich den alten Teichdamm kreuzte.

Plötzlich schoss ein unheimliches Licht quer über den Pfad, und ich blickte zurück, um zu sehen, woher ein so ungewöhnlicher Glanz kommen könne, denn hinter mir lagen allein das weite

The radiance was that of the full, setting, and blood-red moon which now shone vividly through that once barely-discernible fissure of which I have before spoken as extending from the roof of the building, in a zigzag direction, to the base.

While I gazed, this fissure rapidly widened--there came a fierce breath of the whirlwind--the entire orb of the satellite burst at once upon my sight--my brain reeled as I saw the mighty walls rushing asunder--there was a long tumultuous shouting sound like the voice of a thousand waters--and the deep and dank tarn at my feet closed sullenly and silently over the fragments of the "House of Usher".

Schloss und seine Schatten.

Der Strahl war Mondglanz, und der volle, untergehende, blutrote Mond schien jetzt hell durch den einst kaum wahrnehmbaren Riss, von dem ich bereits früher sagte, dass er vom Dach des Hauses im Zickzack bis zum Erdboden lief.

Während ich hinstarrte, erweiterte sich dieser Riss mit unheimlicher Schnelligkeit; ein wütender Stoß des Wirbelsturms kam; das volle Rund des Satelliten wurde in dem breit aufgerissenen Spalt sichtbar; mein Geist wankte, als ich jetzt die gewaltigen Mauern auseinanderbersten sah; es folgte ein langes tosendes Krachen wie das Getöse von tausend Wasserfällen, und der tiefe und schwarze Teich zu meinen Füßen schloss sich finster und schweigend über den Trümmern des ›Hauses Usher‹.

Die Maske des roten Todes - The Masque of the Red Death

THE "Red Death" had long devastated the country.

No pestilence had ever been so fatal, or so hideous.

Blood was its Avatar and its seal--the redness and the horror of blood.

There were sharp pains, and sudden dizziness, and then profuse bleeding at the pores, with dissolution.

The scarlet stains upon the body and especially upon the face of the victim, were the pest ban which shut him out from the aid and from the sympathy of

Lange schon wütete der ›Rote Tod‹ im Lande;

nie war eine Pest verheerender, nie eine Krankheit grässlicher gewesen.

Blut war der Anfang, Blut das Ende – überall das Rot und der Schrecken des Blutes.

Mit stechenden Schmerzen und Schwindelanfällen setzte es ein, dann quoll Blut aus allen Poren, und das war der Beginn der Auflösung.

Die scharlachroten Tupfen am ganzen Körper der unglücklichen Opfer – und besonders im Gesicht – waren des Roten Todes Bannsiegel, das die Gezeichneten

his fellow-men. And the whole seizure, progress and termination of the disease, were the incidents of half an hour.

But the Prince Prospero was happy and dauntless and sagacious.

When his dominions were half depopulated, he summoned to his presence a thousand hale and light-hearted friends from among the knights and dames of his court, and with these retired to the deep seclusion of one of his castellated abbeys.

This was an extensive and magnificent structure, the creation of the prince's own eccentric yet august taste.

A strong and lofty wall girdled it in. This wall had gates of iron.

The courtiers, having entered, brought furnaces and massy hammers and welded the bolts.

They resolved to leave means neither of ingress or egress to the sudden impulses of despair or of frenzy from within.

The abbey was amply provisioned. With such precautions the courtiers might bid defiance to contagion.

The external world could take care of itself.

In the meantime it was folly to grieve, or to think.

The prince had provided all the appliances of pleasure.

There were buffoons, there were improvisatori, there were ballet-dancers, there were musicians, there was Beauty, there was wine.

von der Hilfe und der Teilnahme ihrer Mitmenschen ausschloss; und alles, vom ersten Anfall bis zum tödlichen Ende, war das Werk einer halben Stunde.

Prinz Prospero aber war fröhlich und unerschrocken und weise.

Als sein Land schon zur Hälfte entvölkert war, erwählte er sich unter den Rittern und Damen des Hofes eine Gesellschaft von tausend heiteren und leichtlebigen Kameraden und zog sich mit ihnen in die stille Abgeschiedenheit einer befestigten Abtei zurück.

Es war dies ein ausgedehnter prächtiger Bau, eine Schöpfung nach des Prinzen eigenem exzentrischen, aber vornehmen Geschmack.

Das Ganze war von einer hohen, mächtigen Mauer umschlossen, die eiserne Tore hatte.

Nachdem die Höflingsschar dort eingezogen war, brachten die Ritter Schmelzöfen und schwere Hämmer herbei und schmiedeten die Riegel der Tore fest.

Es sollte weder für die draußen wütende Verzweiflung noch für ein etwaiges törichtes Verlangen der Eingeschlossenen eine Türe offen sein.

Da die Abtei mit Proviant reichlich versehen war und alle erdenklichen Vorsichtsmaßregeln getroffen worden waren, glaubte die Gesellschaft der Pestgefahr Trotz bieten zu können.

Die Welt da draußen mochte für sich selbst sorgen!

Jedenfalls schien es unsinnig, sich vorläufig bangen Gedanken hinzugeben.

Auch hatte der Prinz für allerlei Zerstreuungen Sorge getragen.

Da waren Gaukler und Komödianten, Musikanten und Tänzer – da war Schönheit und Wein.

All these and security were within. Without was the "Red Death."

It was toward the close of the fifth or sixth month of his seclusion, and while the pestilence raged most furiously abroad, that the Prince Prospero entertained his thousand friends at a masked ball of the most unusual magnificence.

It was a voluptuous scene, that masquerade.

But first let me tell of the rooms in which it was held.

There were seven--an imperial suite.

In many palaces, however, such suites form a long and straight vista, while the folding doors slide back nearly to the walls on either hand, so that the view of the whole extent is scarcely impeded.

Here the case was very different;

as might have been expected from the duke's love of the bizarre. The apartments were so irregularly disposed that the vision embraced but little more than one at a time.

There was a sharp turn at every twenty or thirty yards, and at each turn a novel effect.

To the right and left, in the middle of each wall, a tall and narrow Gothic window looked out upon a closed corridor which pursued the windings of the suite.

These windows were of stained glass whose color varied in accordance with the prevailing hue of the decorations of the chamber into which it opened.

That at the eastern extremity was hung, for example, in blue--and vividly blue

All dies und dazu das Gefühl der Sicherheit war drinnen in der Burg – draußen war der Rote Tod.

Im fünften oder sechsten Monat der fröhlichen Zurückgezogenheit versammelte Prinz Prospero – während draußen die Pest noch mit ungebrochener Gewalt raste – seine tausend Freunde auf einem Maskenball mit unerhörter Pracht.

Reichtum und zügellose Lust herrschten auf dem Feste.

Doch ich will zunächst die Räumlichkeiten schildern, in denen das Fest abgehalten wurde.

Es waren sieben wahrhaft königliche Gemächer.

Im allgemeinen bilden in den Palästen solche Festräume – da die Flügeltüren nach beiden Seiten bis an die Wand zurückgeschoben werden können – eine lange Zimmerflucht, die einen weiten Durchblick gewährt.

Dies war hier jedoch nicht der Fall.

Des Prinzen Vorliebe für alles Absonderliche hatte die Gemächer vielmehr so zusammengegliedert, dass man von jedem Standort immer nur einen Saal zu überschauen vermochte.

Nach Durchquerung jedes Einzelraumes gelangte man an eine Biegung, und jede dieser Wendungen brachte ein neues Bild.

In der Mitte jeder Seitenwand befand sich ein hohes, schmales gotisches Fenster, hinter dem eine schmale Galerie den Windungen der Zimmerreihe folgte.

Diese Fenster hatten Scheiben aus Glasmosaik, dessen Farbe immer mit dem vorherrschenden Farbenton des betreffenden Raumes übereinstimmte.

Das am Ostende gelegene Zimmer zum Beispiel war in Blau gehalten, und so

were its windows.

The second chamber was purple in its ornaments and tapestries, and here the panes were purple.

The third was green throughout, and so were the casements.

The fourth was furnished and lighted with orange--the fifth with white--the sixth with violet.

The seventh apartment was closely shrouded in black velvet tapestries that hung all over the ceiling and down the walls, falling in heavy folds upon a carpet of the same material and hue.

But in this chamber only, the color of the windows failed to correspond with the decorations. The panes here were scarlet--a deep blood color.

Now in no one of the seven apartments was there any lamp or candelabrum, amid the profusion of golden ornaments that lay scattered to and fro or depended from the roof.

There was no light of any kind emanating from lamp or candle within the suite of chambers.

But in the corridors that followed the suite, there stood, opposite to each window, a heavy tripod, bearing a brazier of fire that projected its rays through the tinted glass and so glaringly illumined the room.

And thus were produced a multitude of gaudy and fantastic appearances.

But in the western or black chamber the effect of the fire-light that streamed upon the dark hangings through the blood-tinted panes, was ghastly in the extreme, and produced so wild a look upon the

waren auch seine Fenster leuchtend blau.

Das folgende Gemach war in Wandbekleidung und Ausstattung purpurn, und auch seine Fenster waren purpurn.

Das dritte war ganz in Grün und hatte dementsprechend grüne Fensterscheiben.

Das vierte war orangefarben eingerichtet und hatte orangefarbene Beleuchtung. Das fünfte war weiß, das sechste violett.

Die Wände des siebenten Zimmers aber waren dicht mit schwarzem Sammet bezogen, der sich auch über die Deckenwölbung spannte und in schweren Falten auf einen Teppich von gleichem Stoffe niederfiel.

Und nur in diesem Raume glich die Farbe der Fenster nicht derjenigen der Dekoration: hier waren die Scheiben scharlachrot – wie Blut.

Nun waren sämtliche Gemächer zwar reich an goldenen Ziergegenständen, die an den Wänden entlang standen oder von der Decke herabhingen, kein einziges aber besaß einen Kandelaber oder Kronleuchter.

Es gab weder Lampen- noch Kerzenlicht.

Statt dessen war draußen auf der an den Zimmern hinlaufenden Galerie vor jedem Fenster ein schwerer Dreifuß aufgestellt, der ein kupfernes Feuerbecken trug, dessen Flamme ihren Schein durch das farbige Fenster hereinwarf und so den Raum schimmernd erhellte.

Hierdurch wurden die phantastischsten Wirkungen erzielt.

In dem westlichsten oder schwarzen Gemach aber war der Glanz der Flammenglut, der durch die blutig roten Scheiben in die schwarzen Sammetfalten fiel, so gespenstisch und gab den

countenances of those who entered, that there were few of the company bold enough to set foot within its precincts at all.

It was in this apartment, also, that there stood against the western wall, a gigantic clock of ebony.

Its pendulum swung to and fro with a dull, heavy, monotonous clang; and when the minute-hand made the circuit of the face, and the hour was to be stricken, there came from the brazen lungs of the clock a sound which was clear and loud and deep and exceedingly musical, but of so peculiar a note and emphasis that, at each lapse of an hour, the musicians of the orchestra were constrained to pause, momentarily, in their performance, to hearken to the sound;

and thus the waltzers perforce ceased their evolutions; and there was a brief disconcert of the whole gay company;

and, while the chimes of the clock yet rang, it was observed that the giddiest grew pale, and the more aged and sedate passed their hands over their brows as if in confused reverie or meditation.

But when the echoes had fully ceased, a light laughter at once pervaded the assembly;

the musicians looked at each other and smiled as if at their own nervousness and folly, and made whispering vows, each to the other, that the next chiming of the clock should produce in them no similar emotion;

and then, after the lapse of sixty minutes, (which embrace three thousand and six hundred seconds of the Time that flies,) there came yet another chiming of the

Gesichtern der hier Eintretenden ein derart erschreckendes Aussehen, dass nur wenige aus der Gesellschaft kühn genug waren, den Fuß über die Schwelle zu setzen.

In diesem Gemach befand sich an der westlichen Wand auch eine hohe Standuhr in einem riesenhaften Ebenholzkasten.

Ihr Pendel schwang mit dumpfem, wuchtigem, eintönigem Schlag hin und her; und wenn der Minutenzeiger seinen Kreislauf über das Zifferblatt beendet hatte und die Stunde schlug, so kam aus den ehernen Lungen der Uhr ein voller, tiefer, sonorer Ton, dessen Klang so sonderbar ernst und so feierlich war, dass bei jedem Stundenschlag die Musikanten des Orchesters, von einer unerklärlichen Gewalt gezwungen, ihr Spiel unterbrachen, um diesem Ton zu lauschen.

So musste der Tanz plötzlich aussetzen, und eine kurze Missstimmung befiel die heitere Gesellschaft.

So lange die Schläge der Uhr ertönten, sah man selbst die Fröhlichsten erbleichen, und die Älteren und Besonneneren strichen mit der Hand über die Stirn, als wollten sie wirre Traumbilder oder unliebsame Gedanken verscheuchen.

Kaum aber war der letzte Nachhall verklungen, so durchlief ein lustiges Lachen die Versammlung.

Die Musikanten schämten sich lächelnd ihrer Empfindsamkeit und Torheit, und flüsternd vereinbarten sie, dass der nächste Stundenschlag sie nicht wieder derart aus der Fassung bringen solle.

Allein wenn nach wiederum sechzig Minuten (dreitausendsechshundert Sekunden der flüchtigen Zeit) die Uhr von neuem anschlug, trat dasselbe

clock, and then were the same disconcert and tremulousness and meditation as before.

But, in spite of these things, it was a gay and magnificent revel.

The tastes of the duke were peculiar.

He had a fine eye for colors and effects.

He disregarded the decora of mere fashion.

His plans were bold and fiery, and his conceptions glowed with barbaric lustre.

There are some who would have thought him mad.

His followers felt that he was not.

It was necessary to hear and see and touch him to be sure that he was not.

He had directed, in great part, the moveable embellishments of the seven chambers, upon occasion of this great fete; and it was his own guiding taste which had given character to the masqueraders.

Be sure they were grotesque.

There were much glare and glitter and piquancy and phantasm--much of what has been since seen in "Hernani."

There were arabesque figures with unsuited limbs and appointments. There were delirious fancies such as the madman fashions.

There was much of the beautiful, much of the wanton, much of the bizarre, something of the terrible, and not a little of that which might have excited disgust.

To and fro in the seven chambers there stalked, in fact, a multitude of dreams.

allgemeine Unbehagen ein, dasselbe Bangen und Sinnen wie vordem.

Doch wenn man hiervon absah, war es eine prächtige Lustbarkeit.

Der Prinz hatte einen eigenartigen Geschmack bewiesen.

Er hatte ein feines Empfinden für Farbenwirkungen.

Alles Herkömmliche und Modische war ihm zuwider,

er hatte seine eigenen kühnen Ideen, und seine Phantasie liebte seltsame glühende Bilder.

Es gab Leute, die ihn für wahnsinnig hielten.

Sein Gefolge aber wusste, dass er es nicht wahr.

Doch man musste ihn sehen und kennen, um dessen gewiss zu sein.

Die Einrichtung und Ausschmückung der sieben Gemächer war eigens für dieses Fest ganz nach des Prinzen eigenen Angaben gemacht worden, und sein eigener merkwürdiger Geschmack hatte auch den Charakter der Maskerade bestimmt.

Gewiss, sie war grotesk genug.

Da gab es viel Prunkendes und Glitzerndes, viel Phantastisches und Pikantes.

Da gab es Masken mit seltsam verrenkten Gliedmaßen, die Arabesken vorstellen sollten, und andere, die man nur mit den Hirngespinsten eines Wahnsinnigen vergleichen konnte.

Es gab viel Schönes und viel Üppiges, viel Übermütiges und viel Groteskes, und auch manch Schauriges – aber nichts, was irgendwie widerwärtig gewirkt hätte.

In der Tat, es schien, als wogten in den sieben Gemächern eine Unzahl von

Träumen durcheinander.

And these--the dreams--writhed in and about, taking hue from the rooms, and causing the wild music of the orchestra to seem as the echo of their steps.

And, anon, there strikes the ebony clock which stands in the hall of the velvet. And then, for a moment, all is still, and all is silent save the voice of the clock.

The dreams are stiff-frozen as they stand.

But the echoes of the chime die away-- they have endured but an instant--and a light, half-subdued laughter floats after them as they depart.

And now again the music swells, and the dreams live, and writhe to and fro more merrily than ever, taking hue from the many-tinted windows through which stream the rays from the tripods.

But to the chamber which lies most westwardly of the seven, there are now none of the maskers who venture; for the night is waning away; and there flows a ruddier light through the blood-colored panes; and the blackness of the sable drapery appals;

and to him whose foot falls upon the sable carpet, there comes from the near clock of ebony a muffled peal more solemnly emphatic than any which reaches their ears who indulge in the more remote gaieties of the other apartments.

But these other apartments were densely crowded, and in them beat feverishly the heart of life.

And the revel went whirlingly on, until at length there commenced the sounding of midnight upon the clock.

Und diese Träume wanden sich durch die Säle, deren jeder sie mit seinem besonderen Licht umspielte, und die tollen Klänge des Orchesters schienen wie ein Echo ihres Schreitens.

Von Zeit zu Zeit aber riefen die Stunden der schwarzen Riesenuhr in dem Sammetsaal, und eine kurze Weile herrschte eisiges Schweigen – nur die Stimme der Uhr erdröhnte.

Die Träume erstarrten.

Doch das Geläut verhallte – und ein leichtes halbunterdrücktes Lachen folgte seinem Verstummen.

Die Musik rauschte wieder, die Träume belebten sich von neuem und wogten noch fröhlicher hin und her, farbig beglänzt durch das Strahlenlicht der Flammenbecken, das durch die vielen bunten Scheiben strömte.

Aber in das westliche der sieben Gemächer wagte sich jetzt niemand mehr hinein, denn die Nacht war schon weit vorgeschritten, und greller noch floss das Licht durch die blutroten Scheiben und überflammte die Schwärze der düsteren Draperien;

wer den Fuß hier auf den dunklen Teppich setzte, dem dröhnte das dumpfe, schwere Atmen der nahen Riesenuhr warnender, schauerlicher ins Ohr als allen jenen, die sich in der Fröhlichkeit der anderen Gemächer umhertummelten.

Diese anderen Räume waren überfüllt, und in ihnen schlug fieberheiß das Herz des Lebens.

Und der Trubel rauschte lärmend weiter, bis endlich die ferne Uhr den Zwölfschlag der Mitternacht erschallen ließ.

And then the music ceased, as I have told; and the evolutions of the waltzers were quieted; and there was an uneasy cessation of all things as before.

But now there were twelve strokes to be sounded by the bell of the clock; and thus it happened, perhaps, that more of thought crept, with more of time, into the meditations of the thoughtful among those who revelled.

And thus, too, it happened, perhaps, that before the last echoes of the last chime had utterly sunk into silence, there were many individuals in the crowd who had found leisure to become aware of the presence of a masked figure which had arrested the attention of no single individual before.

And the rumor of this new presence having spread itself whisperingly around, there arose at length from the whole company a buzz, or murmur, expressive of disapprobation and surprise--then, finally, of terror, of horror, and of disgust.

In an assembly of phantasms such as I have painted, it may well be supposed that no ordinary appearance could have excited such sensation.

In truth the masquerade license of the night was nearly unlimited; but the figure in question had out-Heroded Herod, and gone beyond the bounds of even the prince's indefinite decorum.

There are chords in the hearts of the most reckless which cannot be touched without emotion. Even with the utterly lost, to whom life and death are equally jests, there are matters of which no jest can be made.

The whole company, indeed, seemed now deeply to feel that in the costume and bearing of the stranger neither wit

Und die Musik verstummte, so wie früher; und der Tanz wurde jäh zerrissen, und wie früher trat ein plötzlicher unheimlicher Stillstand ein.

Jetzt aber musste der Schlag der Uhr zwölfmal ertönen; und daher kam es, dass jenen, die in diesem Kreis die Nachdenklichen waren, noch trübere Gedanken kamen, und dass ihre Versonnenheit noch länger andauerte.

Und daher kam es wohl auch, dass, bevor noch der letzte Nachhall des letzten Stundenschlages erstorben war, manch einer Muße genug gefunden hatte, eine Maske zu bemerken, die bisher noch keinem aufgefallen war.

Das Gerücht von dieser neuen Erscheinung sprach sich flüsternd herum, und es erhob sich in der ganzen Versammlung ein Summen und Murren des Unwillens und der Entrüstung – das schließlich zu Lauten des Schreckens, des Entsetzens und höchsten Abscheus anwuchs.

Man kann sich denken, dass es keine gewöhnliche Erscheinung war, die den Unwillen einer so toleranten Gesellschaft erregen konnte.

Man hatte in dieser Nacht der Maskenfreiheit zwar sehr weite Grenzen gezogen, doch die fragliche Gestalt war in der Tat zu weit gegangen – über des Prinzen weitgehende Duldsamkeit hinaus.

Auch in den Herzen der Übermütigsten gibt es Saiten, die nicht berührt werden dürfen, und selbst für die Verstocktesten, denen Leben und Tod nur Spiel ist, gibt es Dinge, mit denen sie nicht Scherz treiben lassen.

Einmütig schien die Gesellschaft zu empfinden, dass in Tracht und Benehmen der befremdenden Gestalt

nor propriety existed.

The figure was tall and gaunt, and shrouded from head to foot in the habiliments of the grave.

The mask which concealed the visage was made so nearly to resemble the countenance of a stiffened corpse that the closest scrutiny must have had difficulty in detecting the cheat.

And yet all this might have been endured, if not approved, by the mad revellers around.

But the mummer had gone so far as to assume the type of the Red Death.

His vesture was dabbled in blood--and his broad brow, with all the features of the face, was besprinkled with the scarlet horror.

When the eyes of Prince Prospero fell upon this spectral image (which with a slow and solemn movement, as if more fully to sustain its role, stalked to and fro among the waltzers) he was seen to be convulsed, in the first moment with a strong shudder either of terror or distaste; but, in the next, his brow reddened with rage.

"Who dares?" he demanded hoarsely of the courtiers who stood near him--"who dares insult us with this blasphemous mockery?

Seize him and unmask him--that we may know whom we have to hang at sunrise, from the battlements!"

It was in the eastern or blue chamber in which stood the Prince Prospero as he uttered these words.

They rang throughout the seven rooms loudly and clearly--for the prince was a bold and robust man, and the music had

weder Witz noch Anstand sei.

Lang und hager war die Erscheinung, von Kopf zu Fuß in Leichentücher gehüllt.

Die Maske, die das Gesicht verbarg, war dem Antlitz eines Toten täuschend nachgebildet. Selbst die dichteste Prüfung würde es schwer haben den Betrug aufzudecken.

Und doch, all dieses hätten die tollen Gäste des tollen Gastgebers, wenn es ihnen auch nicht gefiel, noch hingehen lassen.

Aber der Verwegene war so weit gegangen, die Gestalt des ›Roten Todes‹ darzustellen.

Sein Gewand war mit Blut besudelt, und seine breite Stirn, das ganze Gesicht sogar, war mit dem scharlachroten Todesspiegel gefleckt.

Als die Blicke des Prinzen Prospero diese Gespenstergestalt entdeckten, die, um ihre Rolle noch wirkungsvoller zu spielen, sich langsam und feierlich durch die Reihen der Tanzenden bewegte, sah man, wie er im ersten Augenblick von einem Schauer des Entsetzens oder des Widerwillens geschüttelt wurde; im nächsten Moment aber rötete sich seine Stirn in Zorn.

"Wer wagt es", fragte er mit heiserer Stimme die Höflinge an seiner Seite, "wer wagt es, uns durch solch gotteslästerlichen Hohn zu empören?

Ergreift und demaskiert ihn, damit wir wissen, wer es ist, der bei Sonnenaufgang an den Zinnen des Schlosses aufgeknüpft werden wird!"

Es war in dem östlichen, dem blauen Zimmer, in dem Prinz Prospero diese Worte rief.

Sie hallten laut und deutlich durch alle sieben Gemächer – denn der Prinz war ein kräftiger und kühner Mann, und die

become hushed at the waving of his hand.

It was in the blue room where stood the prince, with a group of pale courtiers by his side.

At first, as he spoke, there was a slight rushing movement of this group in the direction of the intruder, who at the moment was also near at hand, and now, with deliberate and stately step, made closer approach to the speaker.

But from a certain nameless awe with which the mad assumptions of the mummer had inspired the whole party, there were found none who put forth hand to seize him;

so that, unimpeded, he passed within a yard of the prince's person; and, while the vast assembly, as if with one impulse, shrank from the centres of the rooms to the walls, he made his way uninterruptedly, but with the same solemn and measured step which had distinguished him from the first,

through the blue chamber to the purple--through the purple to the green--through the green to the orange--through this again to the white--and even thence to the violet, ere a decided movement had been made to arrest him.

It was then, however, that the Prince Prospero, maddening with rage and the shame of his own momentary cowardice, rushed hurriedly through the six chambers, while none followed him on account of a deadly terror that had seized upon all.

He bore aloft a drawn dagger, and had approached, in rapid impetuosity, to within three or four feet of the retreating figure, when the latter, having attained the extremity of the velvet apartment,

Musik war durch eine Bewegung seiner Hand zum Schweigen gebracht worden.

Das blaue Zimmer war es, in dem der Prinz stand, umgeben von einer Gruppe bleicher Höflinge.

Sein Befehl brachte Bewegung in die Höflingsschar, als wolle man den Eindringling angreifen, der gerade jetzt ganz in der Nähe war und mit würdevoll gemessenem Schritt dem Sprecher näher trat.

Doch das namenlose Grauen, das die wahnwitzige Vermessenheit des Vermummten allen eingeflößt hatte, war so stark, dass keiner die Hand ausstreckte, um ihn aufzuhalten.

Ungehindert kam er bis dicht an den Prinzen heran – und während die zahlreiche Versammlung zu Tode entsetzt zur Seite wich und sich in allen Gemächern bis an die Wand zurückdrängte, ging er unangefochten seines Weges, mit den nämlichen feierlichen und gemessenen Schritten wie zu Beginn.

Und er schritt von dem blauen Zimmer in das purpurrote – von dem purpurroten in das grüne – von dem grünen in das orangefarbene – und aus diesem in das weiße – und weiter noch in das violette Zimmer, ehe eine entscheidende Bewegung gemacht wurde, um ihn aufzuhalten.

Dann aber war es Prinz Prospero, der rasend vor Zorn und Scham über seine eigene unbegreifliche Feigheit die sechs Zimmer durcheilte – er allein, denn von den andern vermochte infolge des tödlichen Schreckens kein einziger ihm zu folgen.

Den Dolch in der erhobenen Hand war er in wildem Ungestüm der weiterschreitenden Gestalt bis auf drei oder vier Schritte nahe gekommen, als diese, die jetzt das Ende des

turned suddenly and confronted his pursuer.

There was a sharp cry--and the dagger dropped gleaming upon the sable carpet, upon which, instantly afterwards, fell prostrate in death the Prince Prospero.

Then, summoning the wild courage of despair, a throng of the revellers at once threw themselves into the black apartment, and, seizing the mummer, whose tall figure stood erect and motionless within the shadow of the ebony clock,

gasped in unutterable horror at finding the grave-cerements and corpse-like mask which they handled with so violent a rudeness, untenanted by any tangible form.

And now was acknowledged the presence of the Red Death.

He had come like a thief in the night.

And one by one dropped the revellers in the blood-bedewed halls of their revel, and died each in the despairing posture of his fall.

And the life of the ebony clock went out with that of the last of the gay.

And the flames of the tripods expired.

And Darkness and Decay and the Red Death held illimitable dominion over all.

Sammetgemaches erreicht hatte, sich plötzlich zurückwandte und dem Verfolger gegenüberstand.

Man hörte einen durchdringenden Schrei, der Dolch fiel blitzend auf den schwarzen Teppich, und im nächsten Augenblick sank auch Prinz Prospero im Todeskampf zu Boden.

Nun stürzten mit dem Mute der Verzweiflung einige der Gäste in das schwarze Gemach und ergriffen den Vermummten, dessen hohe Gestalt aufrecht und regungslos im Schatten der schwarzen Uhr stand.

Doch unbeschreiblich war das Grauen, das sie befiel, als sie in den Leichentüchern und hinter der Leichenmaske, die sie mit rauem Griffe packten, nichts Greifbares fanden – sie waren leer ...

Und nun erkannte man die Gegenwart des Roten Todes.

Er war gekommen wie ein Dieb in der Nacht.

Und einer nach dem andern sanken die Festgenossen in den blutbetauten Hallen ihrer Lust zu Boden und starben – ein jeder in der verzerrten Lage, in der er verzweifelnd niedergefallen war.

Und das Leben in der Ebenholzuhr erlosch mit dem Leben des letzten der Fröhlichen.

Und die Gluten in den Kupferpfannen verglommen.

Und unbeschränkt herrschte über alles mit Finsternis und Verwesung der Rote Tod.

Das Fass Amontillado - The Cask of Amontillado

THE thousand injuries of Fortunato I had borne as I best could; but when he ventured upon insult, I vowed revenge.

Alle die tausend kränkenden Reden Fortunatos ertrug ich, so gut ich konnte, als er aber Beleidigungen und Beschimpfungen wagte, schwor ich ihm Rache.

You, who so well know the nature of my soul, will not suppose, however, that I gave utterance to a threat.

Ihr werdet doch nicht annehmen – ihr, die ihr so gut das Wesen meiner Seele kennt –, dass ich eine Drohung laut werden ließ.

At length I would be avenged;

Einmal würde ich gerächt sein!

this was a point definitively settled--but the very definitiveness with which it was resolved, precluded the idea of risk.

Aber die Bestimmtheit, mit der ich meinen Entschluss fasste, verbot mir alles, was mein Vorhaben gefährden konnte.

I must not only punish, but punish with impunity. A wrong is unredressed when retribution overtakes its redresser.

Ein Unrecht ist nicht bestraft, wenn den Rächer Vergeltung trifft für seine Rachetat;

It is equally unredressed when the avenger fails to make himself felt as such to him who has done the wrong.

es ist auch nicht bestraft, wenn es dem Rächer nicht gelingt, sich als solcher seinem Opfer zu zeigen.

It must be understood, that neither by word nor deed had I given Fortunato cause to doubt my good will.

Es muss vorausgeschickt werden, dass ich Fortunato weder mit Wort noch Tat Grund gegeben, meine gute Gesinnung anzuzweifeln.

I continued, as was my wont, to smile in his face, and he did not perceive that my smile NOW was at the thought of his immolation.

Ich war weiter liebenswürdig zu ihm, und er gewahrte nicht, dass mein Lächeln JETZT dem Gedanken seiner Vernichtung galt.

He had a weak point--this Fortunato--although in other regards he was a man to be respected and even feared.

Er hatte eine Schwäche, dieser Fortunato – obschon er in anderer Hinsicht ein geachteter und sogar gefürchteter Mann war.

He prided himself on his connoisseurship in wine.

Er brüstete sich damit, dass er ein Weinkenner sei.

Few Italians have the true virtuoso spirit.

Nur wenige Italiener besitzen den wahren Kunstverstand.

For the most part their enthusiasm is adopted to suit the time and opportunity--to practise imposture upon the British and Austrian

Sie begeistern sich meist nur für eine einzige Sache: für betrügerische Manipulationen gegenüber britischen und österreichischen MILLIONÄREN.

MILLIONAIRES.

In painting and gemmary, Fortunato, like his countrymen, was a quack--but in the matter of old wines he was sincere.

In this respect I did not differ from him materially: I was skilful in the Italian vintages myself, and bought largely whenever I could.

It was about dusk, one evening during the supreme madness of the carnival season, that I encountered my friend.

He accosted me with excessive warmth, for he had been drinking much.

The man wore motley.

He had on a tight-fitting parti-striped dress, and his head was surmounted by the conical cap and bells.

I was so pleased to see him, that I thought I should never have done wringing his hand.

I said to him--"My dear Fortunato, you are luckily met.

How remarkably well you are looking to-day!

But I have received a pipe of what passes for Amontillado, and I have my doubts."

"How?"

said he. "Amontillado?

A pipe?

Impossible!

And in the middle of the carnival!"

"I have my doubts," I replied;

"and I was silly enough to pay the full Amontillado price without consulting you in the matter.

You were not to be found, and I was fearful of losing a bargain."

In der Beurteilung von Bildern und Edelsteinen war Fortunato, gleich seinen Landsleuten, ein unwissender Prahlhans, in Bezug auf alte Weine aber hatte er ein ehrliches und sicheres Urteil.

Hierin stand ich selbst ihm kaum nach; ich kannte die italienischen Weine gut und kaufte viel, sooft sich mir günstige Gelegenheit bot.

Es war in der tollen Karnevalszeit, als ich an einem dämmerigen Abend meinem Freunde begegnete.

Er begrüßte mich mit übertriebener Wärme, denn er hatte viel getrunken.

Der Mann war maskiert.

Er trug ein enganliegendes, zur Hälfte gestreiftes Gewand, und auf seinem Kopfe erhob sich die konisch geformte Narrenkappe.

Ich freute mich so sehr, ihn zu sehen, dass ich gar kein Ende finden konnte, ihm die Hand zu schütteln.

Ich sagte zu ihm: "Mein lieber Fortunato, es freut mich, dich zu treffen.

Wie prächtig du heute aussiehst – außerordentlich wohl!

Doch höre: ich habe ein Fass Wein bekommen, das für Amontillado gilt, und ich habe meine Zweifel."

"Wie?"

sagte er, "Amontillado?

Ein Fass?

Unmöglich!

Und mitten im Karneval?"

"Ich habe meine Zweifel", erwiderte ich.

"Und ich war töricht genug, den vollen Amontillado-Preis zu zahlen, ohne dich erst zu Rate zu ziehen.

Du warst nicht zu finden, und ich fürchtete, durch eine Verzögerung den ganzen Handel zu verlieren."

"Amontillado!"

"I have my doubts."

"Amontillado!"

"And I must satisfy them."

"Amontillado!"

"As you are engaged, I am on my way to Luchesi.

If any one has a critical turn, it is he.

He will tell me--" "Luchesi cannot tell Amontillado from Sherry."

"And yet some fools will have it that his taste is a match for your own."

"Come, let us go."

"Whither?"

"To your vaults."

"My friend, no; I will not impose upon your good nature.

I perceive you have an engagement.

Luchesi--" "I have no engagement;-- come."

"My friend, no.

It is not the engagement, but the severe cold with which I perceive you are afflicted.

The vaults are insufferably damp.

They are encrusted with nitre."

"Let us go, nevertheless.

The cold is merely nothing.

Amontillado!

You have been imposed upon. And as for Luchesi, he cannot distinguish Sherry from Amontillado."

Thus speaking, Fortunato possessed himself of my arm.

Putting on a mask of black silk, and drawing a roquelaire closely about my

"Amontillado!"

"Ich habe meine Zweifel."

"Amontillado!"

"Und ich muss sie zum Schweigen bringen."

"Amontillado!"

"Da du beschäftigt bist, werde ich Luchesi aufsuchen.

Wenn einer ein kritisches Urteil hat, ist er es.

Er wird mir sagen –" "Luchesi kann Amontillado nicht von Sherry unterscheiden!"

"Und doch behaupten so ein paar Narren, dass sein Weinverstand dem deinigen gleichkomme."

"Komm, lass uns gehen."

"Wohin?"

"In deine Kellereien."

"Nein, mein Freund; ich will nicht deine Gutmütigkeit ausnützen.

Ich sehe, du bist beschäftigt.

Luchesi –" "Ich bin nicht beschäftigt, komm!"

"Lieber Freund, nein!

Es ist ja nicht nur das, dass du etwas anderes vorhattest; du bist ernstlich erkältet.

Die Kellergewölbe sind unerträglich feucht.

Sie haben eine Salpeterkruste angesetzt."

"Lass uns trotzdem gehen!

Die Erkältung ist nicht der Rede wert.

Amontillado!

Man hat dich betrogen; und Luchesi – der kann Sherry von Amontillado nicht unterscheiden."

Mit diesen Worten zog Fortunato mich fort.

Ich nahm eine schwarze Seidenmaske vors Gesicht, hüllte mich dicht in meinen

person, I suffered him to hurry me to my palazzo.

There were no attendants at home; they had absconded to make merry in honor of the time.

I had told them that I should not return until the morning, and had given them explicit orders not to stir from the house.

These orders were sufficient, I well knew, to insure their immediate disappearance, one and all, as soon as my back was turned.

I took from their sconces two flambeaux, and giving one to Fortunato, bowed him through several suites of rooms to the archway that led into the vaults.

I passed down a long and winding staircase, requesting him to be cautious as he followed.

We came at length to the foot of the descent, and stood together on the damp ground of the catacombs of the Montresors.

The gait of my friend was unsteady, and the bells upon his cap jingled as he strode.

"The pipe," said he.

"It is farther on," said I;

"but observe the white web-work which gleams from these cavern walls."

He turned towards me, and looked into my eyes

with two filmy orbs that distilled the rheum of intoxication.

"Nitre?"

he asked, at length. "Nitre," I replied.

"How long have you had that cough?"

"Ugh! ugh! ugh!--ugh! ugh!

Mantel und duldete, dass er mich eilends zu meinem Palazzo geleitete.

Die Dienerschaft war nicht zu Hause; der Karneval hatte sie hinausgelockt.

Ich hatte den Leuten gesagt, dass ich nicht vor dem nächsten Morgen heimkommen würde, und ihnen streng verboten, sich aus dem Hause zu rühren.

Ich wusste, dass dies genügte, damit alle zusammen, sobald ich ihnen den Rücken wandte, davonliefen.

Ich nahm aus den Ringen an der Wand zwei Fackeln, gab Fortunato eine davon und komplimentierte ihn durch mehrere Zimmerreihen in den Bogengang, der zu den Gewölben führte.

Ich schritt eine lange gewundene Treppe hinab und bat ihn, mir vorsichtig zu folgen.

Endlich kamen wir unten an und standen zusammen in der feuchten Tiefe der Katakomben der Montresors.

Der Gang meines Freundes war unsicher, und die Schellen an seiner Kappe klingelten bei jedem Schritt.

"Das Fass!" sagte er.

"Das ist weiter hinten", antwortete ich.

"Siehst du das weiße Gewebe, das da ringsum von den Kellermauern leuchtet?"

Er wandte sich mir zu und sah mir in die Augen.

Seine Blicke waren feucht von Schnupfen und Trunkenheit.

"Salpeter?"

fragte er schließlich. "Salpeter", erwiderte ich.

"Wie lange hast du schon diesen Husten?"

Er hustete, hustete, hustete.

My poor friend found it impossible to reply for many minutes.

"It is nothing," he said, at last.

"Come," I said, with decision, "we will go back; your health is precious.

You are rich, respected, admired, beloved; you are happy, as once I was.

You are a man to be missed.

For me it is no matter.

We will go back;

you will be ill, and I cannot be responsible.

Besides, there is Luchesi--" "Enough," he said; "the cough is a mere nothing; it will not kill me.

I shall not die of a cough."

"True--true," I replied; "and, indeed, I had no intention of alarming you unnecessarily--but you should use all proper caution.

A draught of this Medoc will defend us from the damps."

Here I knocked off the neck of a bottle which I drew from a long row of its fellows that lay upon the mould.

"Drink," I said, presenting him the wine.

He raised it to his lips with a leer.

He paused and nodded to me familiarly, while his bells jingled.

"I drink," he said, "to the buried that repose around us."

"And I to your long life."

He again took my arm, and we proceeded.

"These vaults," he said, "are extensive."

"The Montresors," I replied, "were a great and numerous family."

Mein armer Freund konnte minutenlang keine Antwort geben.

"Es ist nichts", erwiderte er dann.

"Komm", sagte ich sehr bestimmt, "wir wollen umkehren; deine Gesundheit ist kostbar.

Du bist reich, geachtet, bewundert, geliebt; du bist glücklich, wie ich einst war.

Du würdest eine Lücke hinterlassen.

Um mich ist es nicht schade.

Wir wollen umkehren!

Du wirst krank werden, und ich kann das nicht verantworten.

Übrigens kann ja Luchesi –" "Genug!" sagte er. "Der Husten ist ganz belanglos; er wird mich nicht umbringen.

Ich werde nicht daran zugrunde gehen."

"Wahr – wahr", erwiderte ich. "Wirklich, ich hatte nicht die Absicht, dich unnötig zu beunruhigen – aber du solltest die Vorsicht nicht außer acht lassen.

Ein Schluck Médoc wird uns vor der Einwirkung der Dünste schützen."

Bei diesen Worten zog ich aus einer langen Flaschenreihe, die längs der Mauer auf der Erde lag, eine Flasche hervor und schlug ihr den Hals ab.

"Trink", sagte ich und bot ihm den Wein.

Er setzte ihn an die Lippen.

Er hielt inne und nickte mir vertraulich zu; seine Glöckchen klingelten.

"Ich trinke", sagte er, "auf die Toten, die hier unten ruhen."

"Und ich auf dein langes Leben!"

Er nahm von neuem meinen Arm, und wir gingen weiter.

"Diese Gewölbe", sagte er, "sind weitläufig."

"Die Montresors", erwiderte ich, "waren eine große und zahlreiche Familie."

"I forget your arms."

"A huge human foot d'or, in a field azure; the foot crushes a serpent rampant whose fangs are imbedded in the heel."

"And the motto?"

"Nemo me impune lacessit."

"Good!"

he said.

The wine sparkled in his eyes and the bells jingled.

My own fancy grew warm with the Medoc.

We had passed through walls of piled bones, with casks and puncheons intermingling, into the inmost recesses of the catacombs.

I paused again, and this time I made bold to seize Fortunato by an arm above the elbow.

"The nitre!"

I said: "see, it increases.

It hangs like moss upon the vaults.

We are below the river's bed.

The drops of moisture trickle among the bones.

Come, we will go back ere it is too late.

Your cough--" "It is nothing," he said; "let us go on.

But first, another draught of the Medoc."

I broke and reached him a flagon of De Grâve.

He emptied it at a breath.

His eyes flashed with a fierce light.

He laughed and threw the bottle upwards with a gesticulation I did not understand.

"Ich vergaß dein Wappenzeichen."

"Ein riesiger goldener Fuß in blauem Felde; der Fuß zertritt eine sich bäumende Schlange, deren Zähne ihm in der Ferse sitzen."

"Und das Motto?"

"Nemo me impune lacessit."

"Gut!"

sagte er.

Der Wein flackerte aus seinen Augen, und die Glöckchen klingelten.

Auch mir stieg der Médoc zu Kopfe.

Wir waren an einer ganzen Reihe aufgestapelter Skelette und Fässer vorbei bis in den entferntesten Teil der Katakomben gelangt.

Ich blieb wieder stehen, und diesmal wagte ich es, Fortunato am Arm zu rütteln.

"Der Salpeter!"

sagte ich. "Sieh, wie es immer mehr wird.

Er hängt an den Wölbungen wie Moos.

Wir sind unter dem Flussbett.

Die Nässe tropft durch die Skelette.

Komm, wir wollen umkehren, ehe es zu spät ist.

Dein Husten –" "Nicht der Rede wert", sagte er; "lass uns weitergehen.

Vorher aber ... noch einen Schluck Médoc."

Ich schlug einer Flasche de Grave den Hals ab und reichte sie ihm.

Er leerte sie mit einem Zug.

In seinen Augen flackerte ein wildes Licht.

Er lachte und warf die Flasche mit einer seltsamen Bewegung zur Decke – eine Geste, die ich nicht verstand.

I looked at him in surprise.

He repeated the movement--a grotesque one.

"You do not comprehend?"

he said.

"Not I," I replied.

"Then you are not of the brotherhood."

"How?"

"You are not of the masons."

"Yes, yes," I said, "yes, yes."

"You?

Impossible!

A mason?"

"A mason," I replied.

"A sign," he said.

"It is this," I answered, producing a trowel from beneath the folds of my roquelaire.

"You jest," he exclaimed, recoiling a few paces.

"But let us proceed to the Amontillado."

"Be it so," I said, replacing the tool beneath the cloak, and again offering him my arm.

He leaned upon it heavily.

We continued our route in search of the Amontillado.

We passed through a range of low arches, descended, passed on, and descending again, arrived at a deep crypt, in which the foulness of the air caused our flambeaux rather to glow than flame.

At the most remote end of the crypt there appeared another less spacious.

Its walls had been lined with human remains, piled to the vault overhead, in the fashion of the great catacombs of Paris.

Three sides of this interior crypt were still ornamented in this manner.

Ich sah ihn verwundert an.

Er wiederholte die absonderliche Geste.

"Du verstehst nicht?"

fragte er.

"Nicht im geringsten", antwortete ich.

"Du gehörst nicht zur Bruderschaft!"

"Wie?"

"Du bist kein Maurer."

"Ja, ja", sagte ich. "Jawohl, ja."

"Du?

Unmöglich!

Ein Maurer?"

"Ein Maurer", antwortete ich.

"Ein Zeichen!" sagte er.

"Hier ist es", erwiderte ich, aus den Falten meines Überwurfs eine Maurerkelle hervorziehend.

"Du spaßest", rief er aus und wich vor mir zurück.

"Aber komm weiter zum Amontillado!"

"Gut also", sagte ich, nahm die Kelle wieder unten den Mantel und bot ihm den Arm.

Er lehnte sich schwer darauf.

Wir setzten unseren Weg fort.

Wir gingen durch mehrere niedere Bogengänge, gingen hinab, hinauf und wieder hinab, und betraten nun eine tiefe Gruft, wo die Luft so modrig war, dass unsere Fackeln nicht mehr flammten, sondern nur noch schwelten.

Am entlegensten Ende der Gruft kam eine andere, kleinere zum Vorschein.

An ihren Wänden waren bis zur Decke hinauf Menschenknochen aufgestapelt gewesen, ähnlich wie in den großen Katakomben von Paris.

Drei Seiten dieser innersten Gruftkammer waren noch jetzt so

From the fourth the bones had been thrown down, and lay promiscuously upon the earth, forming at one point a mound of some size.

Within the wall thus exposed by the displacing of the bones, we perceived a still interior recess, in depth about four feet, in width three, in height six or seven.

It seemed to have been constructed for no especial use in itself, but formed merely the interval between two of the colossal supports of the roof of the catacombs, and was backed by one of their circumscribing walls of solid granite.

It was in vain that Fortunato, uplifting his dull torch, endeavored to pry into the depths of the recess.

Its termination the feeble light did not enable us to see.

"Proceed," I said; "herein is the Amontillado.

As for Luchesi--" "He is an ignoramus," interrupted my friend, as he stepped unsteadily forward, while I followed immediately at his heels.

In an instant he had reached the extremity of the niche, and finding his progress arrested by the rock, stood stupidly bewildered.

A moment more and I had fettered him to the granite.

In its surface were two iron staples, distant from each other about two feet, horizontally.

From one of these depended a short chain, from the other a padlock.

Throwing the links about his waist, it was but the work of a few seconds to

geschmückt.

Von der vierten waren die Knochen weggeräumt; sie lagen auf dem Boden herum und waren an einer Stelle zu einem Haufen aufgetürmt.

Inmitten der so bloßgelegten Mauer bemerkten wir noch eine letzte Höhlung. Sie war etwa vier Fuß tief, drei Fuß breit und sechs bis sieben Fuß hoch.

Sie schien nicht zu irgendeinem besonderen Zwecke gemacht worden zu sein, sondern bildete lediglich den Zwischenraum zwischen drei der mächtigen Stützpfeiler, die die Deckenwölbung der Katakomben trugen; ihre Rückwand wurde von einer der massiven Granitmauern gebildet.

Vergeblich hob Fortunato seine trübe Fackel, um in die Tiefe der Höhlung zu spähen.

Das schwache Licht gestattete nicht, die Rückwand zu erblicken.

"Geh weiter", sagte ich. "Hier drin ist der Amontillado.

Übrigens könnte Luchesi –" "Er ist ein Dummkopf", fiel mir mein Freund ins Wort, während er unsicher vorwärts schritt; ich folgte ihm auf den Fersen.

Einen Augenblick später hatte er das Ende der Höhlung erreicht; verdutzt stand er vor der Mauer, die ihm Halt gebot.

Und noch einen Augenblick später hatte ich ihn an den Granit gefesselt.

In der Mauer befanden sich auf gleicher Höhe und in zwei Fuß Entfernung voneinander zwei Schließhaken; an einem derselben hing eine kurze Kette, am andern ein Vorlegeschloss.

Ich warf die Kette um Fortunatos Leib und befestigte sie im Schloss.

Das Ganze war das Werk weniger Sekunden.

secure it.

He was too much astounded to resist.	Er war zu verblüfft, um Widerstand entgegenzusetzen.
Withdrawing the key I stepped back from the recess.	Ich zog den Schlüssel ab und trat aus der Nische zurück.
"Pass your hand," I said,	"Streich mit der Hand über die Mauer", sagte ich.
"over the wall; you cannot help feeling the nitre.	"Du wirst den Salpeter fühlen.
Indeed it is VERY damp.	Wahrhaftig, es ist SEHR feucht darin.
Once more let me IMPLORE you to return.	Noch einmal: lass dich BESCHWÖREN, umzukehren!
No?	Nein?
Then I must positively leave you.	Dann muss ich dich wirklich verlassen.
But I must first render you all the little attentions in my power."	Aber zuerst muss ich dir noch alle die kleinen Aufmerksamkeiten erweisen, die in meiner Macht stehen."
"The Amontillado!"	"Der Amontillado!"
ejaculated my friend, not yet recovered from his astonishment.	rief mein Freund, der sich von seinem Erstaunen noch nicht erholt hatte.
"True," I replied; "the Amontillado."	"Wahr", erwiderte ich; "der Amontillado."
As I said these words I busied myself among the pile of bones of which I have before spoken.	Bei diesen Worten machte ich mir am Knochenhaufen zu schaffen, von dem ich vorhin gesprochen habe.
Throwing them aside, I soon uncovered a quantity of building stone and mortar.	Ich warf die Knochen beiseite und legte bald eine Anzahl Bausteine und ein Häufchen Mörtel bloß.
With these materials and with the aid of my trowel, I began vigorously to wall up the entrance of the niche.	Mit diesen Materialien und mit Hilfe der Maurerkelle begann ich, eilig den Eingang der Nische zuzumauern.
I had scarcely laid the first tier of my masonry when I discovered that the intoxication of Fortunato had in a great measure worn off.	Ich hatte kaum die erste Reihe des Mauerwerks errichtet, als ich entdeckte, dass Fortunatos Betrunkenheit sehr nachgelassen hatte.
The earliest indication I had of this was a low moaning cry from the depth of the recess.	Das erste Anzeichen dafür gab mir ein leiser klagender Schrei, der aus der Tiefe der Höhlung kam.
It was NOT the cry of a drunken man.	Es war NICHT der Schrei eines Betrunkenen.
There was then a long and obstinate silence.	Dann folgte ein langes eigensinniges Schweigen.

I laid the second tier, and the third, and the fourth; and then I heard the furious vibrations of the chain.

The noise lasted for several minutes, during which, that I might hearken to it with the more satisfaction, I ceased my labors and sat down upon the bones.

When at last the clanking subsided, I resumed the trowel, and finished without interruption the fifth, the sixth, and the seventh tier.

The wall was now nearly upon a level with my breast.

I again paused, and holding the flambeaux over the mason-work, threw a few feeble rays upon the figure within.

A succession of loud and shrill screams, bursting suddenly from the throat of the chained form, seemed to thrust me violently back.

For a brief moment I hesitated--I trembled.

Unsheathing my rapier, I began to grope with it about the recess: but the thought of an instant reassured me.

I placed my hand upon the solid fabric of the catacombs, and felt satisfied.

I reapproached the wall.

I replied to the yells of him who clamored.

I re-echoed--I aided--I surpassed them in volume and in strength.

I did this, and the clamorer grew still.

It was now midnight, and my task was drawing to a close.

I had completed the eighth, the ninth,

Ich mauerte eine zweite Reihe – und eine dritte und vierte; und dann hörte ich das wütende Stoßen und Schwingen der festgespannten Kette.

Das Geräusch dauerte mehrere Minuten, während welcher ich, um besser lauschen zu können, meine Arbeit einstellte und mich auf den Knochenhaufen setzte.

Als das hastige Klirren endlich aufhörte, ergriff ich von neuem die Kelle und vollendete ohne Unterbrechung die fünfte, die sechste und die siebente Reihe.

Der Wall war nun fast in gleicher Höhe mit meiner Brust.

Ich hielt von neuem inne, hob die Fackel über das Mauerwerk und warf damit ein paar schwache Strahlen auf die Gestalt da drinnen.

Da stieß der Gefesselte plötzlich wilde Schreie aus – viele laute gellende Schreie, die mich zurücktaumeln machten.

Einen Augenblick zögerte ich – zitterte ich.

Ich zog den Degen und stach damit in das Dunkel der Nische hinein. Doch nach kurzer Überlegung beruhigte ich mich wieder.

Ich legte die Hand auf das massige Gemäuer der Katakomben und war befriedigt.

Ich trat wieder an meine Mauer.

Ich antwortete auf das Geheul des Rufenden.

Ich ahmte es nach – verstärkte es – übertönte es.

Das tat ich eine Weile, und der Schreier wurde still.

Es war jetzt Mitternacht, und meine Arbeit nahte sich ihrem Ende.

Ich hatte die achte, die neunte und die

and the tenth tier.

I had finished a portion of the last and the eleventh; there remained but a single stone to be fitted and plastered in.

I struggled with its weight;

I placed it partially in its destined position.

But now there came from out the niche a low laugh that erected the hairs upon my head.

It was succeeded by a sad voice, which I had difficulty in recognising as that of the noble Fortunato.

The voice said-- "Ha! ha! ha!--he! he!--a very good joke indeed--an excellent jest. We will have many a rich laugh about it at the palazzo--he! he! he!--over our wine--he! he! he!"

"The Amontillado!"

I said.

"He! he! he!--he! he! he!--yes, the Amontillado.

But is it not getting late?

Will not they be awaiting us at the palazzo, the Lady Fortunato and the rest?

Let us be gone."

"Yes," I said, "let us be gone."

"For the love of God, Montressor!"

"Yes," I said, "for the love of God!"

But to these words I hearkened in vain for a reply.

I grew impatient. I called aloud-- "Fortunato!"

No answer.

I called again-- "Fortunato!"

No answer still.

I thrust a torch through the remaining aperture and let it fall within.

zehnte Reihe vollendet.

Ich hatte einen Teil der elften und letzten Reihe beendet; es blieb nur noch ein einziger Stein einzusetzen und festzumauern.

Ich rang mit seinem Gewicht.

Ich hob ihn an seinen Platz, konnte ihm jedoch nicht sogleich eine richtige Lage geben.

Jetzt kam aus der Nische ein leises Lachen, das mir die Haare auf dem Kopf zu Berge stehen machte.

Dann sprach eine traurige Stimme, die ich nur schwer als die Stimme des edlen Fortunato erkennen konnte.

Die Stimme sagte: "Ha ha ha – he he – wahrhaftig ein guter Spaß, wir werden im Palazzo noch oft darüber lachen – he he he – über unsern Wein – he he he!"

"Den Amontillado!"

sagte ich.

"He he he – – he he – ja, den Amontillado.

Aber ist es nicht schon spät?

Werden sie uns nicht im Palazzo erwarten? Die Lady Fortunato und die andern?

Lass uns gehen."

"Ja", sagte ich, "lass uns gehen."

"Bei der Liebe Gottes, Montresor!"

"Ja", sagte ich, "bei der Liebe Gottes!"

Aber auf diese Worte erwartete ich vergeblich eine Antwort.

Ich wurde ungeduldig, ich rief laut: "Fortunato!"

Keine Antwort.

Ich rief wieder: "Fortunato!"

Noch keine Antwort.

Ich nahm seine Fackel, stieß sie durch die Öffnung und ließ sie drinnen zu

Boden fallen.

There came forth in return only a jingling of the bells.

Als Antwort kam nur ein Klingeln der Schellen.

My heart grew sick--on account of the dampness of the catacombs.

Mein Herz wurde schwer – infolge der Moderluft in den Katakomben.

I hastened to make an end of my labor.

Ich beeilte mich, meine Arbeit zu beenden.

I forced the last stone into its position; I plastered it up.

Ich zwang den letzten Stein in seine richtige Lage. Ich mauerte ihn ein.

Against the new masonry I re-erected the old rampart of bones.

Gegen das neue Mauerwerk türmte ich den alten Knochenwall auf.

For the half of a century no mortal has disturbed them.

Seit einem halben Jahrhundert hat kein Sterblicher ihn angerührt.

In pace requiescat!

In pace requiescat!

Das schwatzende Herz - The Tell-Tale Heart

TRUE!--nervous--very, very dreadfully nervous I had been and am;

WAHR ist es: nervös, entsetzlich nervös war ich damals und bin es noch.

but why will you say that I am mad?

Warum aber müsst ihr durchaus behaupten, dass ich wahnsinnig sei?

The disease had sharpened my senses-- not destroyed--not dulled them.

Mein nervöser Zustand hatte meinen Verstand nicht zerrüttet, sondern ihn geschärft, hatte meine Sinne nicht abgestumpft, sondern wachsamer gemacht.

Above all was the sense of hearing acute.

Vor allem hatte sich mein Gehörsinn wunderbar fein entwickelt.

I heard all things in the heaven and in the earth.

Ich hörte alle Dinge im Himmel und auf Erden.

I heard many things in hell.

Ich hörte viele Dinge in der Hölle.

How, then, am I mad? Hearken!

Und das sollte Wahnsinn sein?

and observe how healthily--how calmly I can tell you the whole story.

Hört zu und merkt auf, wie sachlich, wie ruhig ich die ganze Geschichte erzählen kann.

It is impossible to say how first the idea entered my brain; but once conceived, it haunted me day and night.

Ich kann nicht sagen, wann der Gedanke mich zum erstenmal überfiel. Er war urplötzlich da und verfolgte mich Tag und Nacht.

Object there was none.

Passion there was none.
I loved the old man.
He had never wronged me.
He had never given me insult.
For his gold I had no desire.

I think it was his eye!
yes, it was this!
He had the eye of a vulture--a pale blue eye, with a film over it.

Whenever it fell upon me, my blood ran cold;
and so by degrees--very gradually--I made up my mind to take the life of the old man, and thus rid myself of the eye forever.

Now this is the point.
You fancy me mad.
Madmen know nothing.
But you should have seen me.
You should have seen how wisely I proceeded--with what caution--with what foresight--with what dissimulation I went to work!
I was never kinder to the old man than during the whole week before I killed him.
And every night, about midnight, I turned the latch of his door and opened it--oh so gently!
And then, when I had made an opening sufficient for my head, I put in a dark lantern, all closed, closed, that no light shone out, and then I thrust in my head.

Oh, you would have laughed to see how

Ein wichtiges Motiv war nicht vorhanden.
Hass war nicht vorhanden.
Ich liebte den alten Mann.
Er hatte mir nie etwas zuleid getan.
Er hatte mir nie eine Kränkung zugefügt.
Nach seinem Geld trug ich kein Verlangen.

Ich glaube, es war sein Auge.
Ja, das war es!
Eins seiner Augen glich vollständig dem Auge eines Geiers – ein blasses blaues Auge mit einem Häutchen darüber.

Wann immer es mich anblickte, erstarrte mir das Blut.
Und so – nach und nach – immer zwingender – setzte sich der Gedanke in mir fest, dem alten Mann das Leben zu nehmen und mich auf diese Weise für immer von dem Auge zu befreien.

Nun merkt wohl auf!
Ihr haltet mich für verrückt.
Verrückte erwägen nichts.
Aber mich hättet ihr sehen sollen!
Ihr hättet sehen sollen, wie klug ich vorging – mit wieviel Vorsicht – mit wieviel Umsicht – mit wieviel Heuchelei ich zu Werke ging!
Ich war nie freundlicher zu dem alten Mann als während der ganzen Woche, bevor ich ihn umbrachte.
Und jede Nacht gegen Mitternacht drückte ich auf seine Türklinke und öffnete die Tür – oh, so leise!
Und dann, wenn der Spalt weit genug war, dass ich den Kopf hindurchstecken konnte, hielt ich eine verdunkelte, ganz geschlossene Laterne ins Zimmer; sie war ganz geschlossen, so dass kein Lichtschein herausdrang. Und dann folgte mein Kopf.

Oh, ihr hättet gelacht, wenn ihr gesehen

cunningly I thrust it in!

I moved it slowly--very, very slowly, so that I might not disturb the old man's sleep.

It took me an hour to place my whole head within the opening so far that I could see him as he lay upon his bed.

Ha! would a madman have been so wise as this?

And then, when my head was well in the room, I undid the lantern cautiously--oh, so cautiously -- cautiously (for the hinges creaked)--I undid it just so much that a single thin ray fell upon the vulture eye.

And this I did for seven long nights--every night just at midnight--but I found the eye always closed; and so it was impossible to do the work; for it was not the old man who vexed me, but his Evil Eye.

And every morning, when the day broke, I went boldly into the chamber, and spoke courageously to him, calling him by name in a hearty tone, and inquiring how he has passed the night.

So you see he would have been a very profound old man, indeed, to suspect that every night, just at twelve, I looked in upon him while he slept.

Upon the eighth night I was more than usually cautious in opening the door.

A watch's minute hand moves more quickly than did mine.

Never before that night had I felt the extent of my own powers--of my sagacity.

hättet, wie geschickt ich ihn vorstreckte!

Ich bewegte ihn ganz langsam vorwärts, um nicht den Schlaf des alten Mannes zu stören.

Ich brauchte eine Stunde dazu, den Kopf so weit durch die Öffnung zu schieben, dass ich den Alten in seinem Bette sehen konnte.

Ha! wäre ein Wahnsinniger wohl so weise vorgegangen?

Und dann, wenn ich meinen Kopf glücklich im Zimmer hatte, öffnete ich vorsichtig die Laterne – oh, so vorsichtig! Ganz sachte, denn die Scharniere kreischten, öffnete ich sie so weit, dass ein einziger feiner Strahl auf das Geierauge fiel.

Und das tat ich sieben Nächte lang, jede Nacht gerade um Mitternacht. Aber ich fand das Auge immer geschlossen, und so war es unmöglich, das Werk zu vollenden; denn es war nicht der alte Mann, der mich ärgerte, sondern sein Scheelauge.

Und jeden Morgen, wenn der Tag anbrach, ging ich kühn zu ihm hinein und sprach mit ihm. Ich nannte ihn munter und herzlich beim Namen und fragte ihn, ob er eine gute Nacht verbracht habe.

Ihr seht also, er hätte wirklich ein sehr schlauer Mann sein müssen, um zu vermuten, dass ich allnächtlich um zwölf Uhr, während er schlief, zu ihm hereinsah.

In der achten Nacht ging ich beim Öffnen der Tür mit ganz besonderer Vorsicht zu Werke.

Der Minutenzeiger einer Uhr rückt gewiss schneller voran, als damals meine Hand.

Niemals vor dieser Nacht hatte ich die Größe meiner Macht, meines Scharfsinns so gefühlt.

I could scarcely contain my feelings of triumph.

To think that there I was, opening the door, little by little, and he not even to dream of my secret deeds or thoughts.

I fairly chuckled at the idea; and perhaps he heard me; for he moved on the bed suddenly, as if startled.

Now you may think that I drew back-- but no.

His room was as black as pitch with the thick darkness, (for the shutters were close fastened, through fear of robbers,) and so I knew that he could not see the opening of the door, and I kept pushing it on steadily, steadily.

I had my head in, and was about to open the lantern, when my thumb slipped upon the tin fastening, and the old man sprang up in bed, crying out--"Who's there?"

I kept quite still and said nothing.

For a whole hour I did not move a muscle, and in the meantime I did not hear him lie down.

He was still sitting up in the bed listening;--just as I have done, night after night, hearkening to the death watches in the wall.

Presently I heard a slight groan, and I knew it was the groan of mortal terror.

It was not a groan of pain or of grief--oh, no! -

it was the low stifled sound that arises from the bottom of the soul when overcharged with awe.

I knew the sound well.

Many a night, just at midnight, when all

Ich konnte kaum meinen Triumph unterdrücken.

Da war ich nun hier und öffnete ganz sacht, ganz allmählich die Tür – und ihm träumte nicht einmal von meinem geheimen Tun und Denken.

Ich kicherte bei diesem Gedanken, und vielleicht hörte er mich, denn er rührte sich – wie erschreckt.

Jetzt könntet ihr denken, ich sei zurückgefahren. Aber nein!

Sein Zimmer war ganz dunkel, denn er hatte die Fensterladen aus Furcht vor Einbrechern fest geschlossen; es war pechschwarz. Und ich wusste also, dass er das Öffnen der Tür nicht sehen konnte, und ich fuhr fort, sie langsam, langsam aufzumachen.

Ich war mit dem Kopf im Zimmer und machte mich daran, die Laterne zu öffnen; da glitt mein Daumen an dem Blechverschluss ab, und der alte Mann schrak im Bett empor und schrie: "Wer ist da?"

Ich verhielt mich ganz still und sagte nichts.

Eine volle Stunde lang rührte ich kein Glied, und in dieser ganzen Zeit hörte ich nicht, dass er sich wieder niederlegte.

Er saß noch aufrecht im Bett und horchte – gerade so, wie ich Nacht um Nacht auf das Ticken der Totenuhren an den Stubenwänden gehorcht habe.

Da hörte ich ein leises Ächzen, und ich wusste, das war das Ächzen tödlichen Entsetzens.

So stöhnte nicht Schmerz und nicht Kummer – o nein! es war das Grauen!

Das war der dumpfe, erstickte Laut, der aus den Tiefen der Seele kommt, wenn das Grauen sie gepackt hält.

Ich kannte diesen Laut gut.

In mancher Nacht, gerade um

the world slept, it has welled up from my own bosom, deepening, with its dreadful echo, the terrors that distracted me.

I say I knew it well.

I knew what the old man felt, and pitied him, although I chuckled at heart.

I knew that he had been lying awake ever since the first slight noise, when he had turned in the bed.

His fears had been ever since growing upon him.

He had been trying to fancy them causeless, but could not.

He had been saying to himself--"It is nothing but the wind in the chimney--it is only a mouse crossing the floor," or "It is merely a cricket which has made a single chirp."

Yes, he had been trying to comfort himself with these suppositions: but he had found all in vain.

All in vain; because Death, in approaching him had stalked with his black shadow before him, and enveloped the victim.

And it was the mournful influence of the unperceived shadow that caused him to feel--although he neither saw nor heard-- to feel the presence of my head within the room.

When I had waited a long time, very patiently, without hearing him lie down, I resolved to open a little--a very, very little crevice in the lantern.

So I opened it--you cannot imagine how stealthily, stealthily--until, at length a simple dim ray, like the thread of the spider, shot from out the crevice and fell full upon the vulture eye.

Mitternacht wenn alle Welt schlief war er aus meiner eigenen Brust heraufgequollen und hatte mit seinem schrecklichen Klang das Entsetzen, das mich von Sinnen brachte, noch vermehrt.

Ich sage, ich kannte diesen ächzenden Laut gut.

Ich wusste, was der alte Mann fühlte, und ich bemitleidete ihn, obschon ich innerlich kicherte.

Ich wusste, dass er wach gelegen, schon seit dem ersten schwachen Geräusch, das ihn aufgeschreckt hatte.

Seitdem war seine Angst von Minute zu Minute gewachsen.

Er hatte versucht, sie als grundlos anzusehen, aber es gelang ihm nicht.

Er hatte sich gesagt: "Es ist weiter nichts als der Wind im Schornstein", oder: "Es ist nur eine Maus, die durchs Zimmer läuft", oder: "Es ist nur eine Grille, die ein einziges Mal gezirpt hat."

Ja, er hatte versucht, sich mit diesen Vermutungen zu beruhigen; aber es war alles vergebens gewesen.

Alles vergebens, weil der nahende Tod schon vor ihn hingetreten war und sein Opfer mit schwarzem Schatten umhüllte.

Und die dunkle Gewalt des unsichtbaren Schattens war es, die ihn – obschon er weder sah noch hörte – fühlen ließ, dass mein Kopf im Zimmer war.

Nachdem ich lange Zeit sehr geduldig gewartet hatte, ohne doch zu hören, dass er sich wieder niederlegte, beschloss ich endlich, einen kleinen – einen winzig kleinen Spalt der Laterne zu öffnen.

Ich begann also – ihr könnt euch gar nicht vorstellen, wie bedachtsam, wie leise – die Laterne zu öffnen, bis schließlich ein einziger matter, spinnfadenfeiner Strahl herausdrang und

auf das Geierauge fiel.

It was open--wide, wide open--and I grew furious as I gazed upon it.

Es war offen, weit offen, und ich wurde rasend, als ich daraufhin starrte.

I saw it with perfect distinctness--all a dull blue, with a hideous veil over it

Ich sah es mit vollkommener Deutlichkeit: nichts als ein stumpfes Blau mit einem ekelhaften Schleier darüber.

that chilled the very marrow in my bones; but I could see nothing else of the old man's face or person: for I had directed the ray as if by instinct, precisely upon the damned spot.

Ich erschauerte bis ins Mark. Aber ich konnte von des alten Mannes Gesicht und Gestalt nichts weiter sehen, denn ich hatte den Strahl wie instinktiv ganz genau auf die verfluchte Stelle gerichtet.

And have I not told you that what you mistake for madness is but over-acuteness of the sense?--now, I say, there came to my ears a low, dull, quick sound, such as a watch makes when enveloped in cotton.

Und nun – habe ich euch nicht gesagt, dass das, was ihr für Wahnsinn haltet, nur eine Überfeinerung der Sinne ist? – nun, sage ich, vernahm mein Ohr ein leises, dumpfes, schnelles Geräusch, ein Geräusch wie das Ticken einer Uhr, die man mit einem Tuch umwickelt hat.

I knew that sound well, too.

Auch diesen Laut kannte ich gut.

It was the beating of the old man's heart.

Es war des alten Mannes Herz, das so schlug.

It increased my fury, as the beating of a drum stimulates the soldier into courage.

Es steigerte meine Wut, wie das Schlagen einer Trommel den Soldaten zu mutigerem Vorgehen anreizt.

But even yet I refrained and kept still.

Aber selbst jetzt bezwang ich mich und blieb still.

I scarcely breathed.

Ich atmete kaum.

I held the lantern motionless.

Ich hielt die Laterne regungslos.

I tried how steadily I could maintain the ray upon the eve.

Ich versuchte den Strahl so beständig wie möglich auf das Auge zu heften.

Meantime the hellish tattoo of the heart increased.

Inzwischen steigerte sich das höllische Trommeln des Herzens.

It grew quicker and quicker, and louder and louder every instant.

Es wurde jede Minute schneller und schneller und lauter und lauter.

The old man's terror must have been extreme!

Das Entsetzen des alten Mannes muss furchtbar gewesen sein.

It grew louder, I say, louder every moment!--do you mark me well I have told you that I am nervous: so I am.

Das Klopfen wurde lauter, sage ich, lauter von Minute zu Minute! – Hört ihr mich wohl? Ich habe euch gesagt, dass ich nervös sei, und das bin ich.

And now at the dead hour of the night, amid the dreadful silence of that old

Und nun, in so toter Nachtstunde, in diesem alten Hause, das so grauenhaft

68

house, so strange a noise as this excited me to uncontrollable terror.

Yet, for some minutes longer I refrained and stood still.

But the beating grew louder, louder!

I thought the heart must burst.

And now a new anxiety seized me--the sound would be heard by a neighbour!

The old man's hour had come!

With a loud yell, I threw open the lantern and leaped into the room.

He shrieked once--once only.

In an instant I dragged him to the floor, and pulled the heavy bed over him.

I then smiled gaily, to find the deed so far done.

But, for many minutes, the heart beat on with a muffled sound.

This, however, did not vex me; it would not be heard through the wall.

At length it ceased.

The old man was dead.

I removed the bed and examined the corpse.

Yes, he was stone, stone dead.

I placed my hand upon the heart and held it there many minutes.

There was no pulsation.

He was stone dead.

His eye would trouble me no more.

If still you think me mad, you will think so no longer when I describe the wise precautions I took for the concealment of the body.

schweigsam war, erweckte dies eine seltsame Geräusch in mir ein maßloses Entsetzen.

Doch noch einige Minuten länger bezwang ich mich und stand still.

Aber das Klopfen wurde lauter und lauter!

Ich dachte, das Herz müsse zerspringen.

Und nun fasste mich eine neue Angst: das Geräusch könnte von einem Nachbarn vernommen werden!

Da war des Alten Stunde gekommen!

Mit einem lauten Geheul riss ich die Blendlaterne auf und sprang ins Zimmer.

Er schrie auf – nur ein einziges Mal!

Im Augenblick zerrte ich ihn auf den Boden hinunter und zog das schwere Federbett über ihn.

Dann lächelte ich, froh, die Tat so weit vollbracht zu sehen.

Aber noch viele Minuten hörte ich den erstickten Laut des klopfenden Herzens.

Das kümmerte mich jedoch nicht. Das konnte nicht durch die Wände hindurch gehört werden.

Endlich hörte es auf.

Der alte Mann war tot.

Ich entfernte das Bett und untersuchte den Leichnam.

Ja, er war tot – tot wie ein Stein.

Ich legte ihm meine Hand aufs Herz und ließ sie minutenlang da liegen.

Kein Pulsschlag war zu spüren.

Er war endgültig tot.

Sein Auge würde mich nicht mehr belästigen.

Solltet ihr mich noch immer für wahnsinnig halten, so werdet ihr eure Anschauung sicher ändern, wenn ich euch schildere, welch kluge Vorsichtsmaßregeln ich ergriff, um den Leichnam zu verbergen.

The night waned, and I worked hastily, but in silence.

First of all I dismembered the corpse. I cut off the head and the arms and the legs.

I then took up three planks from the flooring of the chamber, and deposited all between the scantlings.

I then replaced the boards so cleverly, so cunningly, that no human eye--not even his--could have detected any thing wrong.

There was nothing to wash out--no stain of any kind--no blood-spot whatever.

I had been too wary for that. A tub had caught all--ha! ha!

When I had made an end of these labors, it was four o'clock--still dark as midnight.

As the bell sounded the hour, there came a knocking at the street door.

I went down to open it with a light heart,--for what had I now to fear?

There entered three men, who introduced themselves, with perfect suavity, as officers of the police.

A shriek had been heard by a neighbour during the night; suspicion of foul play had been aroused; information had been lodged at the police office, and they (the officers) had been deputed to search the premises.

I smiled,--for what had I to fear?

I bade the gentlemen welcome.

The shriek, I said, was my own in a dream.

The old man, I mentioned, was absent in the country.

I took my visitors all over the house.

Die Nacht schwand hin, und ich arbeitete eilig, aber in großer Stille.

Aus dem Fußboden des Zimmers hob ich drei Dielen heraus und bereitete darunter dem Toten sein Grab.

Dann legte ich die Bretter wieder an Ort und Stelle.

So geschickt, so sorgfältig tat ich dies, dass kein menschliches Auge – nicht einmal das seine – irgend etwas Auffallendes hätte bemerken können.

Da gab es nichts wegzuwaschen – keinen Fleck irgendwelcher Art – nicht das kleinste Bluttröpfchen.

Dafür war ich viel zu bedachtsam vorgegangen.

Als ich mit dieser Arbeit fertig war, war es vier Uhr – noch immer schwarz wie Mitternacht.

Als die Turmuhr die Stunde anschlug, pochte es am Haustor.

Ich ging leichten Herzens hinunter, um zu öffnen – denn was hatte ich jetzt zu fürchten?

Es traten drei Männer herein, die sich sehr liebenswürdig als Polizeibeamte vorstellten.

Ein Nachbar hatte in der Nacht einen Schrei vernommen; man hatte Verdacht gefasst, hatte dem Polizeiamt Mitteilung gemacht, und sie, die drei Beamten, waren abgesandt worden, um nach der Ursache zu forschen.

Ich lächelte – denn was hatte ich zu fürchten?

Ich hieß die Herren willkommen.

Den Schrei, sagte ich, hätte ich selbst ausgestoßen, in einem Traum.

Der alte Mann sei abwesend, sei aufs Land gereist, bemerkte ich.

Ich führte die Besucher durchs ganze Haus.

I bade them search--search well.

I led them, at length, to his chamber.

I showed them his treasures, secure, undisturbed.

In the enthusiasm of my confidence, I brought chairs into the room, and desired them here to rest from their fatigues, while I myself, in the wild audacity of my perfect triumph, placed my own seat upon the very spot beneath which reposed the corpse of the victim.

The officers were satisfied.

My manner had convinced them.

I was singularly at ease.

They sat, and while I answered cheerily, they chatted of familiar things.

But, ere long, I felt myself getting pale and wished them gone.

My head ached, and I fancied a ringing in my ears: but still they sat and still chatted.

The ringing became more distinct:--It continued and became more distinct:

I talked more freely to get rid of the feeling: but it continued and gained definiteness--until, at length, I found that the noise was not within my ears.

No doubt I now grew VERY pale;--but I talked more fluently, and with a heightened voice.

Yet the sound increased -- and what could I do?

It was a low, dull, quick sound--much such a sound as a watch makes when enveloped in cotton.

I gasped for breath--and yet the officers heard it not.

I talked more quickly--more vehemently;

Ich bat sie, sich umzusehen – gut umzusehen.

Ich führte sie schließlich in sein Zimmer.

Ich zeigte ihnen seine Wertsachen vollzählig und unberührt.

Begeistert über meine Gewissensruhe brachte ich Stühle herbei und ersuchte die Herren, sich hier von ihrer Ermüdung zu erholen, während ich, im Bewusstsein meines vollständigen Sieges, voll ausgelassener Kühnheit meinen eigenen Stuhl genau dorthin stellte, wo unter den Dielen der Leichnam des Opfers ruhte.

Die Beamten waren zufrieden.

Mein Benehmen hatte sie überzeugt.

Ich war ungewöhnlich aufgeräumt.

Sie saßen also, und während ich fröhlich Antwort gab, plauderten sie von privaten Angelegenheiten.

Aber nicht lange, da fühlte ich, dass ich erbleichte, und ich wünschte sie fort.

Mein Kopf schmerzte, und ich glaubte, Ohrensausen zu haben; aber noch immer saßen sie da und plauderten.

Das Sausen wurde deutlicher – es hörte nicht auf und wurde immer deutlicher.

Ich sprach noch unbefangener, um das seltsame Gefühl loszuwerden. Aber es blieb und nahm zu an Deutlichkeit – bis mir endlich klar wurde, dass das Geräusch nicht in den Ohren selbst war.

Zweifellos: jetzt wurde ich sehr bleich – aber ich redete noch eifriger und mit erhobener Stimme.

Doch das Geräusch wurde lauter – und was konnte ich tun?

Es war ein leises, dumpfes, schnelles Geräusch – ein Geräusch wie das Ticken einer Uhr, die man mit einem Tuch umwickelt hat.

Ich rang nach Atem – und dennoch – die Beamten hörten es noch immer nicht.

Ich sprach schneller – heftiger, aber das

but the noise steadily increased.

Geräusch wuchs beständig.

I arose and argued about trifles, in a high key and with violent gesticulations; but the noise steadily increased.

Ich stand auf und redete gereizt und zornig; meine Stimme war schrill, und ich gestikulierte wild – aber das Geräusch wuchs beständig.

Why would they not be gone?

Warum gingen sie denn nicht?

I paced the floor to and fro with heavy strides, as if excited to fury by the observations of the men--but the noise steadily increased.

Ich lief mit wuchtigen Schritten auf und ab, als ob mich die Reden der Männer in Wut gebracht hätten – aber das Geräusch nahm fortwährend zu.

Oh God! what could I do?

O Gott! Was konnte ich tun?

I foamed--I raved--I swore!

Ich schäumte – ich raste – ich fluchte!

I swung the chair upon which I had been sitting, and grated it upon the boards, but the noise arose over all and continually increased.

Ich ergriff den Stuhl, auf dem ich gesessen, und kratzte damit auf den Dielen hin und her – aber das Geräusch erhob sich über alles und nahm fortgesetzt zu.

It grew louder -- louder -- louder!

Es wurde lauter – lauter – lauter!

And still the men chatted pleasantly, and smiled.

Und immer noch plauderten die Männer freundlich und lächelten.

Was it possible they heard not?

War es möglich, dass sie nicht hörten?

Almighty God! -

Allmächtiger Gott!

no, no! They heard!--

– nein, nein! Sie hörten!

they suspected!--they knew!--

– sie argwöhnten! – sie wussten!

they were making a mockery of my horror!-

Sie trieben Spott mit meinem Entsetzen!

this I thought, and this I think.

– Das war es, was ich dachte, und das denke ich noch.

But anything was better than this agony!

Aber alles andere war besser als diese Pein.

Anything was more tolerable than this derision!

Alles war erträglicher als dieser Hohn.

I could bear those hypocritical smiles no longer!

Ich konnte dies heuchlerische Lächeln nicht länger ertragen.

I felt that I must scream or die!

Ich fühlte, dass ich hinausschreien musste – oder sterben!

and now – again! - hark! louder!

– Und jetzt – wieder! – horch!

Louder! louder! louder!

Lauter! lauter! lauter!

"Villains!"

"Schurken!"

I shrieked, "dissemble no more!

kreischte ich, "verstellt euch nicht länger!

I admit the deed!--	Ich bekenne die Tat!
tear up the planks! here, here!--	– Reißt die Dielen auf! – Hier, hier!
It is the beating of his hideous heart!"	– Es ist das Schlagen dieses fürchterlichen Herzens."

Please send an email to **maisonusher@forum-sprachen-lernen.com** with the subject "**Usher En-De**" to receive:

- **a download link for a free audiobook**

- **the Anki Deck for learning the most important vocabulary**.

We will not pass on your contact information to a third party.

The audiobook helps you to listen to the story repeatedly. **This way, you quickly enhance your listening comprehension, pronunciation as well as expand the vocabulary on the go**.

You liked the book, and it proved helpful? Please provide us with feedback; it would be much appreciated. Even if your review is comprised of just one or two sentences, it would help us tremendously.

If you want to further improve your language skills, other books using the same alignment are:

English – French:

The Picture of Dorian Gray (with Audio) (Mystery, Psychological Thriller)

The Snow Queen (Fairy Tale by H.C. Andersen)

English – German:

The Red-Headed League (A Sherlock Holmes mystery)

Alice in Wonderland (Children's classic book)

The Wonderful Adventures of Nils (Adventure of Nils Holgersson with the wild geese)

The Snow Queen (Fairy Tale by H.C. Andersen)

The Picture of Dorian Gray (Mystery, Psychological Thriller)

A Christmas Carol (Classic world literature by Charles Dickens)

English – Italian

Alice in Wonderland (Children's classic book)

Made in the USA
Las Vegas, NV
15 October 2022

57381767R00044